CATCH FISH

in Australia

BRUCE HARRIS has always loved fishing. Born in Adelaide, he caught his first fish, a salmon, from the Grange jetty in June 1935, and went on to fish the jetties and shores of St Vincent Gulf with an old rangoon cane rod, hand-made wooden centrepin reel and Irish linen line. After many years of experience as a commercial fisherman, Bruce founded the very successful boating and fishing pages of the Adelaide *News*.

A keen sportsman, Bruce represented South Australia in numerous yachting titles and, as Cadet Master of Grange Sailing Club, trained budding sailors for 10 years. During the boom in recreational boating and fishing, his lectures have helped hundreds to fully enjoy this past-time.

Author of three guide books and a chart on fishing, he was the first to design a stick-on rule for the legal lengths of fish. Bruce has fished all waters from Tasmania to Darwin, but says his biggest thrill was catching a 7-kg Brown Trout in Tasmania's Lake Pedder only a year after the lake was filled.

How to
CATCH
FISH

in Australia

LANSDOWNE

Bruce Harris

ACKNOWLEDGEMENTS

The photographs throughout this book were contributed by the following:
David Gwyther, Marine Science Laboratory: p. 9 (Barramundi).

Rudie H. Kuiter: p. 11 (Australian Bass); p. 19 (Drummer Bream); p. 21 (Callop); p. 23 (European Carp); p. 25 (Freshwater Catfish); p. 35 (Crayfish); p. 39 (Dhufish); p. 73 (Dusky Morwong); p. 79 (Yellow-eye Mullet); p. 89 (Redfin Perch); p. 91 (Silver Perch); p. 127 (Brown Trout); p. 147 (Yabbies).

Weldon Trannies/Ray Joyce: p. 13 (Blackfish); p. 17 (Bream); p. 31 (Rock Cod); p. 33 (Blue Crabs); p. 41 (Red Emperor); p. 43 (Flathead); p. 45 (Flounder); p. 47 (Garfish); p. 49 (Groper); p. 51 (Gurnard); p. 53 (Hussar); p. 55 (John Dory); p. 61 (Leatherjacket); p. 63 (Lingfish); p. 67 (Horse Mackerel); p. 71 (Blue Morwong); p. 75 (Red Mullet); p. 81 (Mulloway); p. 83 (Nannygai); p. 85 (Parrot Fish); p. 87 (Red Perch); p. 95 (Salmon); p. 99 (Sergeant Baker); p. 105 (Snapper); p. 109 (Squid); p. 111 (Sweep); p. 113 (Sweetlip); p. 115 (Tailor); p. 117 (Tarwhine); p. 119 (Teraglin); p. 121 (Threadfin); p. 129 (Coral Trout); p. 133 (Trumpeter); p. 135 (Tuna); p. 137 (Turrum); p. 145 (Weed Whiting).

Weldon Trannies: p. 15 (Bonito); p. 27 (Sea Catfish); p. 29 (Murray Cod); p. 57 (Black Kingfish); p. 59 (Yellowtail Kingfish); p. 65 (Blue Mackerel); p. 69 (Spanish Mackerel); p. 77 (Jumping Mullet); p. 93 (Queenfish); p. 125 (Trevally); p. 131 (Rainbow Trout); p. 141 (Sand Whiting).

Neville Coleman, Australasian Marine Photographic Index: p. 37 (Dart); p. 97 (Samson Fish).

Peter Moulton, Marine Science Laboratory: p. 103 (School Shark).

L. Morley: p. 107 (Snook); p. 123 (Tommy Ruff); p. 139 (King George Whiting); p. 143 (Silver Whiting).

Shane Mensforth: p. 101 (Cocktail Shark).

South Australian Dept. of Fisheries: p. 7 (Barracouta).

Ben Cropp: p. 5 (Barracuda).

Published by Lansdowne Publishing Pty Ltd
Level 5, 70 George Street, Sydney NSW 2000, Australia

First published by Rigby Publishers in 1988
Reprinted 1992
Reprinted by Lansdowne Publishing Pty Ltd 1994

© Copyright Bruce Harris 1988
Wholly designed and typeset in Australia
Printed in Singapore by Kyodo Printing Co (S'pore) Pte Ltd

National Library of Australia Cataloguing-in-Publication data

Harris, Bruce, 1930-   .
    How to catch fish in Australia.

    Includes index.
    ISBN 1 86302 275 9.

    1. Fishing — Australia. 2. Cookery (Fish). I. Title.

799.10994

Contents

Introduction

How to Catch Fish has been designed to help the amateur fisherman and the housewife. The 72 fish described can be bought in the Australian marketplace and all can be caught from boat and shore. This is not a book for the purist, even though some of the hints can help such people to better their fishing skills.

One brand of rod and reel has been recommended throughout, and is available in tackle shops in Australia. This was done to make it easy for the angler, to avoid the necessity of seeking through a complex list of brands to find the right equipment. Your local stockist will advise you on suitable alternatives.

The recipes are basic and simple, but they will give the housewife the opportunity to cook fish in different ways.

Fishing Tips

The most important thing a new angler can learn is to 'think like a fish'. This is not hard if you put your mind to it.

First, remember that the lives of most sea creatures evolve around the phases of the moon. These phases cause our tides and, in turn, dictate the feeding patterns of many fish. Fish rarely bite well on a fast-flowing tide. This is because their natural food source—small crabs, shrimp, worms, and the like—are well hidden for fear of being washed away in the fast-flowing water. As the tide slows down, they come out to feed and other, bigger fish come in to feed on them. This applies to nearly all of the bottom-feeding fish like whiting, snapper, trevally and flathead.

If the area has long, sandy beaches, the time to fish for mullet, sand whiting, garfish, and tommy ruff is an hour before the turn of the high tide. Again, natural feed is the reason for their presence. During low tide many small shellfish and worms will have died from the heat of the sun and this is what the fish are coming in to feed upon.

With fish like snook (pike), barracouta, salmon, and blue mackerel, a weather change is the main factor which causes them to bite furiously. They all have wind bags which fill and deflate with atmospheric pressure. As the glass drops this bag deflates and this leaves more room in the stomach for food. Therefore, fish for these species on a falling glass, but keep an eye on the weather.

Another thing which will help you understand fish more is to fully inspect the gut of the fish you have caught. Besides the bait which it has already stolen from you, there could be all sorts of other sea creatures and weeds in the stomach. Keep a note of it, and next time you are out try to use a bait which is the same or similar. In addition, always use baits which pertain to an area. If there are plenty of squid about, use it; if worms, use them.

Always keep the baits as soft as possible on the hooks. In most cases a fish likes to 'mouth a bait' before taking it. As it does this you will feel a light pick on the line and nothing more. By the way, the bite you feel on the line is not a bite at all. It is caused by the fish's tail action as it swims away with the bait. Another tip is to check the beaches after a storm, as this will give you valuable information on the type of bottom off the foreshore.

Above all, keep full records: phase of the moon, the weather, sea conditions, clear or dirty water, and how many fish. Fish like snapper, whiting, snook, tommy ruff, garfish, and many others come back to the same areas at the same time each year. If you know when that is, you are halfway there in getting a more-than-average catch.

From now on, start thinking like a fish.

Barracouta

LOCATION

Victoria, Tasmania, South Australia, and parts of Western Australia.

DESCRIPTION

A long and slender silver body with big back fins and a large head. The male has three huge teeth and the female five. Not to be confused with barracuda or gemfish, which is its shorter, thicker cousin.

BAIT

Whole fish like tommy ruff, garfish, small mackerel, and salmon trout, or lures. In most cases, lures like a big silver wobbler are just as good as bait.

GEAR

Shore fishermen should use a surf rod similar to the Silstar 1100 120BWM and a heavy reel like the EX2170. The line should be about 10-kg breaking strain. Boat fishermen should use a Silstar 110066BWJ and an EX2150 reel. A barracouta hand line is similar to a snook line—a heavy 40-kg breaking strain main line with a 10-kg trace, but a further 50-cm wire trace added. All rigs should have a short wire trace. The hooks should be about 6/0 limerick, as the barracouta has a big mouth and the sides are very brittle. Only a few barrel sinker leads are needed, as most of the barracouta are caught near the surface.

HOW TO CATCH

In most cases, the barracouta is caught in the cooler months, but in some areas such as Kangaroo Island they are there all year round. From the shore it is a cast-and-retrieve situation, using a whole fish. Try using the new Comstock cable baiter with its 6/0 hook for fastening the bait. This is a simple device. Another method is to fit the

bait about 2 metres under a big bob float, and let the wave action keep moving the bait.

From a boat the trolling speed should be about 2 knots and the line kept about 3 or 4 metres under the surface. A paravane can be used successfully.

Wear gloves when using a hand line. Once the fish is hooked, take care. Lift it into the boat well away from other people. It will snap at anything and its big, sharp teeth can cause a nasty wound or even take a finger off. Have a mallet handy and give it a sharp blow to the head.

Barracouta are blood fish and should be bled immediately. To do this, place a finger behind the gills and break the blood vessel which runs near the backbone. Lift the tail up and all of the blood will drain out in a few seconds.

HOW TO COOK

Place thick fillets of barracouta in a greased baking dish and sprinkle them with orange juice, paprika, black pepper, and salt. Cover each fillet with breadcrumbs and add a little butter. Bake for about 15 minutes in a 200°C oven. Cover with grated cheese and return to oven until cheese melts. Serve with mashed potatoes, peas and a few baby carrots.

Barracuda

LOCATION

The east coast of Australia, Victoria, Tasmania, South Australia, Western Australia, and parts of the Northern Territory.

BAIT

Strips of fish flesh like salmon, mackerel, or garfish, or whole small fish like tommy ruff. Heavy silver lures can also be used successfully.

DESCRIPTION

Blue-grey on the upper part of the body with a long spiny fin. The head is similar to the barracouta with large eyes and razor-sharp teeth.

GEAR

Use a Silstar 1100-66BWJ fitted with an AT2570 reel. The line should be about 8-kg breaking strain fitted with ganged number 4/0 limerick hooks on a wire trace.

HOW TO CATCH

Barracuda are generally school fish which run near the edge of the Continental Shelf around Australia. However, they do venture into shallower waters and this is where the amateur can pick them up by trolling. They will attack anything that moves and strike with lightning speed. It has even been claimed that they have seriously injured humans at times when schooling in the tropics.

The angler can either troll at about 3 knots with the baited lines about 30 metres astern, or drift and cast and retrieve.

The baits, if fillets are used, should resemble the shape of a fish as near as possible, but be sure that the grain of the fillet runs down to the tail of the bait.

Use a landing net when getting the fish aboard and wear thick gloves. Have a mallet handy to strike the fish on the head as soon as it is aboard. Bleed the fish immediately by cutting the throat. Always store the fish which you have caught in a cool place, on ice if you have it, as the flesh goes soft very quickly.

HOW TO COOK

Mix a beer batter about two hours before preparing the meal. This can be self-raising flour, salt and pepper to taste, mixed into a batter with beer. Allow this to stand for about two hours. Coat the barracuda with seasoned flour. Whisk the batter and dip each fillet into it so that it is liberally coated. Deep fry each fillet until a light golden brown. Garnish with parsley and lemon, and serve with chips and salad.

Barramundi

LOCATION

Northern Queensland, Northern Territory, and northern Western Australia.

DESCRIPTION

Deep silver in colour with a small head, big mouth, and thick body.

BAIT

Small mullet, mud hopper, live freshwater shrimp, prawns, and a range of lures including the Nilsmaster.

GEAR

Use a 2-metre rod similar to the Silstar 1280 66BWB and an AX2660 sidecast reel. For the expert, a bait caster reel is also ideal. The line should be about 8-kg breaking strain, and be sure to use a wire trace.

HOW TO CATCH

Two methods are used when catching barramundi, the fighting fish of the north: one is trolling at about 1 knot from a boat, the other casting from the banks of the streams and billabongs.

From the boat, the Nilsmaster range of lures is used successfully. These lures hold a good depth in the water when trolling and can be easily cast and retrieved. However, it is important to take a range of colours as the barramundi changes its likings from day to day. One day it will take a green lure, the next a red, and so on.

When casting from the banks it is important to select the spots carefully. Barramundi like to lie under over-hanging trees, ready to dart out when a fish or your lure goes past. These trees also afford them protection from other predators such as small crocodiles. They are also protected by two layers of thick scales, just like armour-

plate. Their gills are also razor sharp, hence the wire trace.

When using live bait, just cast near the edge of a tree and let the bait slowly sink and swim. Unlike most fish, the barramundi generally runs to deep water when it strikes.

The strike will be fast, vicious, and strong. When you have a strike, set the hooks firmly for the barramundi has a hard, bony mouth, and be ready for the run. The reel drag should have been already set well below the breaking strain of the line. The fish will stand on its tail and shake its head in its efforts to throw the hook, so just keep weight on the line. A loose line means a lost fish when it comes to barramundi.

Do not pump the fish with the rod; just keep the tip up and let it do its work. Keep winding on the reel, and as the fish tires gradually increase the drag. With a big barramundi this could take up to half an hour, but with patience you will get the fish. As it nears the bank, use a gaff or landing net. Do not try to lift it on the line.

HOW TO COOK

Take a whole barramundi and clean it thoroughly. Line the stomach with a whole can of asparagus and pour the remaining liquid into a baking dish with a little cooking oil or butter. Stitch the asparagus firmly in place. Cover the fish with foil and place in a hot oven. About 200°C for about 30 minutes. Garnish with diced cheese pieces and parsley and serve with an Australian salad.

Australian
Bass

LOCATION

Southern Queensland, New South Wales, Victoria, Tasmania, and occasionally in South Australia.

DESCRIPTION

Deep green back with a yellow belly. Small sloping head and a large mouth.

BAIT

Worms, shrimp, grasshoppers, and at times, crickets.

GEAR

A light tipped rod like the Silstar 1100 60BC and an EX2140 sidecast reel is best. Rig with a 3-kg breaking strain line. Use a quill float which is slightly weighted, so that it stands upright in the water. Add a 1-metre trace with a single number 3 beak hook.

HOW TO CATCH

The Australian Bass is found in rivers which flow into the sea and are influenced by tides. They like brackish water. The bass is a great little fighter and it is first-class eating.

Cast the line into deep holes near overhanging trees. Work the bait slightly, so that the bait appears to be alive to the fish. When the bass takes the bait it will be with one snap of the jaws.

At the same time it will swim quickly away. Set the hook with a light tug on the line—not too hard or the line will snap and allow the fish to run. Keep the tip of the rod well up, so that the full action of the rod is used. As the fish tires, increase the drag on the reel. Use a landing net to lift the fish from the water.

Another method is to drift down the stream and keep casting near the tree-lined bank. Or cast and let the float keep pace with the boat as it drifts downstream. The best

time to fish for bass is on a falling barometer at dawn and dusk.

HOW TO COOK

Take a bass or bream about 2 kg in weight and cut pockets about 3 cm apart on each side. Put a slice of lemon and a dab of butter in each pocket. Dice about 200 grams of prawns and mix with a cup of breadcrumbs, chopped parsley, lemon juice, and a dash of basil. Fill the stomach of the fish with the mixture and stitch or skewer tight. Heat the oven to 200°C and place the fish in a baking dish. Cover the fish with foil. Test the fish for softness regularly. When nearly cooked remove it from the oven. Pour off any surplus juice and brush with butter. Sprinkle the top of the fish with grated cheese and put it under the griller until the cheese is a golden brown. Rice topped with parsley and carrots makes the ideal partner.

Blackfish

LOCATION

The eastern coast of Australia, Victoria, parts of Tasmania, and South Australia.

DESCRIPTION

A typical surf and rock dweller with a small head and deep body. Dark stripes run down the body.

BAIT

Cockles (pipi), worms, green lettuce weed, shrimp, and whitebait. Finely crushed squid can also be used.

GEAR

From the rocks you will need a surf rod similar to the Silstar 1100 106BF and a top-of-the-range surf reel like the EX2170. In some cases these fish can be caught from boats and for this use a Silstar 1100 70 SBM rod and an EX2150 reel.

HOW TO CATCH

First a word of warning. More anglers in Australia have been drowned trying to catch blackfish from the rocks than any other fish. The fish like the broken water and this makes it dangerous for the angler. Remember, there is no such thing as a freak wave; one in about seven is a big one. If the rocks are wet, you can bet a wave has broken over it recently and even if you are sure you are safe, tie a rope around your waist and secure the other end to a firm rock. Now to the fishing.

Blackfish like to play with baits before taking them, therefore it is essential to use light gear. Line about 5-kg breaking strain is ideal. Fit two number 5 beak hooks to a 2-metre trace with a bob float above. Cast into the most turbulent part of the hole. Hold the rod all the time. Many rods have been lost over the rocks with a hooked

blackfish. From a boat, look for rock pools on the sheltered side of an island or reef.

If you fail to catch a blackfish, the chances are you will end up with a feed of sweep. They inhabit the same areas in the southern states.

Blackfish give a real fight, so be sure that the reel drag is set well under the breaking strain.

The flesh of the blackfish is delicate, but it will soften quickly if it is not kept cool and wet.

HOW TO COOK

Cut slits in the sides of a blackfish and add small pieces of shallot and butter. Put the fish in a baking dish and add a thin layer of cooking oil. Pour a full cup of white wine over the fish and place in an oven at about 200°C. In about 35 minutes, depending on the size of the fish, it is ready for serving with a French salad.

Bonito

LOCATION

The east coast of Australia, Victoria, Tasmania, South Australia, and Western Australia.

DESCRIPTION

This fish has a small head, large thick body with stripes, a fine tail, and fins which lie in grooves on the back and sides of the fish.

BAIT

Bonito are caught mainly by trolling and this makes a wide range of lures ideal. These include silver wobblers, plastic squid, and the like. If fishing with bait, use small fish like tommy ruff attached with two close snooded number 3/0 beak hooks. Always use a heavy swivel and make a 2-m trace of 10-kg breaking strain line.

GEAR

A light Silstar semi-game rod fitted with an AT2590 reel. The line should be about 8-kg breaking strain.

HOW TO CATCH

Bonito are caught in the same way as tuna. However, the boat speed can be reduced to about five knots. Lay the lure or bait on the back of the second stern wave. If the school is near the surface and feeding, which they often do off the east coast of Tasmania in late summer and early autumn, you can drift through the school and cast and retrieve the baits. The bonito can be kept near the boat by chumming with pieces of fish flesh. They are not as wary as tuna and do not sound as quickly when disturbed, but it is still wise not to drive through a school—just pick the fish off the edges.

When the fish is hooked be prepared for a fight. Be sure that the reel drag is set well below the line breaking

strain and have at least 200 metres on the reel. The first run will be fast and violent. After that the fish will put all of its strength on the line to break free of the hook. Take your time and the fish will tire.

Always use a gaff or landing net. Never try to lift the fish on the line, no matter how small. Have a bucket handy so that you can bleed the fish by cutting the throat as soon as possible. This will improve the flavour of the fish.

HOW TO COOK

Bonito is an ideal barbeque fish. Take the bonito fillets and wrap them individually in double foil. Before closing the wrapping sprinkle the fish with salt and add dabs of butter. Wrap securely. Place the fish on a hot barbeque and cook for about five minutes on each side. Test the fish with a fork. It will flake easily when fully cooked.

Bream

LOCATION

Western Australia, southern Queensland, New South Wales, Victoria, Tasmania, and South Australia.

DESCRIPTION

Similar looks to a small snapper with deep silver back, white underbelly, spiny back, and broad tail.

BAIT

Sea worms, shrimp, cockles (pipi), whitebait, and uncooked crayfish.

GEAR

The rod should be light and flexible like the Silstar 1282 66SP. The AT-2540 sidecast reel makes an ideal partner. The line should be no more than 5-kg breaking strain, even less if you are a skilled angler. Use a running sinker, about 30 grams, above a 1-metre trace. I prefer a single number 3 beak hook, however two can be used. I have suggested a 30-gram sliding sinker, but if you can get away with no sinker at all so much the better.

HOW TO CATCH

Black Bream are among the most cautious fish in the sea. They shy away from anything which is not natural. The slightest weight of a sinker on tight line is enough for them to drop a bait. Therefore it is essential that there is plenty of loose line so the fish can pick up the bait and not feel the line.

Before fishing, set the drag on the reel well below the breaking strain of the line, as bream will fight fiercely in the initial stages. When using worms, bait the hook fully but leave a tail of about 3 cm, and when using shrimp slide the hook through the inside of the shrimp from head down to the tail.

The rod should be placed in a bank rod holder and left with plenty of loose line. It should be at a 45-degree angle so that when the fish runs and gets to the end of the loose line, the whip of the rod is enough to sink the hook.

Once the fish is hooked it should be yours if you do not hurry. When it gets near the bank, use a landing net to finalise the catch. **Do not** try to lift it ashore. Remember you are only using light line and it is easily broken.

Bream can be found in practically all of the estuaries and seaboard rivers along the coast. They essentially live in sea water but can survive in near freshwater. In fact, at breeding and spawning time the brackish waters are what they prefer. Dawn and dusk is the best time to fish.

Always carry a variety of baits as one day they will take worms, the next shrimp, and so on. Berley can be used, such as a few opened cockles or pieces of worms and shrimp.

If there are any overhanging trees or deep holes in the river or estuary, fish near them as this is where the bream will lie during the day and feed from at night. Be sure that the bait is always fresh and, in the case of worms, live. The best time to fish for bream is during August and September, but they can be caught in lesser numbers all year round.

HOW TO COOK

Cut slivers in either side of a bream and insert slices of lemon. Prepare a mix of finely diced onion, parsley, breadcrumbs, salt, and pepper. Sprinkle the fish with the mix and place in a baking dish with about half a cup of cooking oil. Cover the fish with a lid or foil. The oven should be about 220°C and the cooking time is about 25 minutes. At the 12-minute mark remove the lid and add more of the mix. Serve with a salad in season.

Drummer
Bream

LOCATION

New South Wales, Victoria, and South Australia.

DESCRIPTION

Deep grey to silver in colour, depending on the size and age of the fish. It has a strong, thick body with heavy sharp spines on the back, and a strong tail.

BAIT

Small pieces of fish, bread or dough, pieces of shrimp, and cockles (pipi).

GEAR

A light Silstar 1100–76BWB rod with an AT2550 sidecast reel. The line should be about 6-kg breaking strain fitted with a single number 3 beak hook. No sinker or swivel is needed.

HOW TO CATCH

The drummer is the bane of many an angler. They can see these big fish under wharves and piers, but they refuse to take a bait. This is where skill and patience comes in. Start feeding the drummer with pieces of bread or whatever you choose for bait. At most times they will take this readily. Increase the size of the berley pieces, until they are big enough to completely cover a hook. Cover the hook and about 1 cm of the line with the bait.

Throw in more berley, but this time drop the baited hook with it and let all of the pieces, including the line, slowly sink.

As the drummer takes the berley it will often get around to the baited hook as well. This fish has a very small mouth, so let the bait get right out of sight before striking.

When you strike, try to head the fish away from the pier. They have a habit of heading straight for the piles. They put up a good fight but tire quickly. Let the rod and reel do the work for the first few minutes. Keep the tip of the rod well up and guide the fish where you want it to go.

HOW TO COOK

The Drummer Bream is not a good eating fish. It has a very smelly gut and the flesh is coarse and strong. However, it does make ideal pet food for the family cat. Clean the fish thoroughly and remove the black lining on the gut.

Boil the fish in a salt-water solution for about 30 minutes, and flake the flesh away from the bones. Pack the flesh in pet-size containers and freeze for later use.

Callop

LOCATION

All states.

DESCRIPTION

Small head and a big body. The upper part of the body is a yellow-silver and the underbelly yellow, hence the alternative name.

BAIT

Tiger worms, small yabbies, freshwater shrimp.

GEAR

Use a 2-metre rod similar to the Silstar 1100–76BWB, and an EX2150 sidecast reel. The line should be about 6-kg breaking strain fitted with two number 3 limerick hooks. A 30-gram pyramid sinker can be used below the hooks, or if the fishing area is tree-lined a bob float 2 metres above the hooks is ideal.

HOW TO CATCH

Callop is caught from as far away as the Finke River, which runs into Lake Eyre, to Innamincka, and all of the rivers south which join the River Murray. It is an excellent eating fish and puts up a good fight when hooked. It prefers the shallow backwaters and creeks to the main stream of the rivers. Because of this, European Carp have had a big effect on its population.

Fish near the reeds and willows. This is where most of the fish will be lying in wait for passing prey. When using worms, leave a good sized tail from the hook so that its wriggling action will attract the fish. However, in most cases in the River Murray system try to shy away from worms for bait, as they are a natural for the carp. Small yabbies and freshwater shrimp are easily the best.

Callop generally have a very light bite. They like to feel the bait while stationary and this means that all the angler will feel is a slight pick. If a bob float is being used it will only slightly bob in the water. However, by this time the fish has generally got the bait well in its mouth. Just lift the line to feel the weight of the fish. If the weight is there, strike hard. The callop is a good fighter, so be sure the reel drag is well set and keep the rod up at all times.

The best time to fish for callop is at dawn and dusk. Always take a variety of bait—shrimp, yabbies, and even some rabbit flesh. Set two rods, one on the bottom and one on the top.

HOW TO COOK

Here is one for the real outdoor type. Take a freshwater callop and wrap it firmly in clay. Do not scale or gut the fish. Light a camp fire and see that there are plenty of coals. Put the fish in the clay on the fire and cover it with coals. Leave it for 90 minutes. Peel off the clay and all of the skin and scales will come with it. Slide off each fillet and salt to taste. The gut will be a tight ball left near the backbone.

European
Carp

LOCATION

Throughout the River Murray–Darling River system and their tributaries.

DESCRIPTION

Small head, large lazy body. The head has two whiskers. They range in colour from near black to gold and silver, with red-tipped fins.

BAIT

Worms mainly, but small yabbies, shrimp, and red meat can be used.

GEAR

A rod about 2 metres in length similar to the Silstar 1280 66BWB and an AX2650 sidecast reel is ideal. Use an 8-kg line. The rig is basic — a star or pyramid sinker below two number 3 limerick hooks. The two hooks set about 2 metres below a bob float can also be used.

HOW TO CATCH

First, it must be remembered that the European Carp is a noxious fish and must not be returned to the water. It must be destroyed immediately, that is killed as soon as it is caught. However, it can give an angler some great sport. They put up a good fight and are listed in many record books.

To catch the carp it must first be learnt that they do not bite like normal fish. They suck in mud from the river banks and through their gill set-up extract the nutrients and expel the rest of the mud, thus polluting a stream. Naturally, worms are the food they normally find. This is why they are best for bait. Cast the line on to the mudflat in a backwater for the best result. This will be where the carp are most prolific.

Leave some loose line and watch it carefully. When it starts to move, strike immediately. If you do not strike straight away, the hook will be well into the stomach and hard to get out. This is a fish which should be destroyed, so do not worry how many you catch, the more the better. They are a great fish for the beginner—a real practice fish. They can be caught at any time of day or night.

HOW TO COOK

Cut the fillets from the European Carp and remove the skin. Soak the fillets in spiced vinegar for a day. This will liquify most of the small bones. Take the fish from the vinegar and soak it for 15 minutes in clean water with a tablespoon of salt. The flesh will then be soft and flakey. Place a layer of the flaked fish in a heat-proof dish and cover the layer with diced onions, parsley, shredded carrots, and capsicum slices. Add another layer of fish. Bake in a warm oven, about 150°C, for about 45 minutes. Take it out and add grated cheese to the top. Replace in the oven for another five minutes.

Freshwater
Catfish

LOCATION

Most inland waters of Australia.

DESCRIPTION

Brown in colour with a big flathead-type head and two whiskers under the mouth. A long, slender tail.

BAIT

Tiger worms, freshwater shrimp, minnows, and small yabbies.

GEAR

A 2-metre rod with a fine tip similar to the Silstar 1280 70BWS and an EX2150 sidecast reel. Use two number 3 beak hooks above a 30-gram pyramid or star sinker.

HOW TO CATCH

The Freshwater Catfish is one which anglers either love or hate. In Darwin they are left on the bank to rot, but in the River Murray system they are sought after. They have good fighting qualities and grow to about 10 kg.

Fish near the reeds and trees in the streams during daylight hours but at night turn to the mud flats. There is no need for the baits to be right on the bottom, as the Freshwater Catfish will rise to a bait. They have a strong bite and a hard mouth, so a very firm strike is needed to set the hook.

Always use a landing net. Like the Sea Catfish, they have poisonous spines near the gills. Wear gloves and remove the head as soon as the fish is landed.

HOW TO COOK

Coat fillets of Freshwater Catfish with seasoned flour and place them in pre-heated oil in a heavy pan. The cooking should only take a few minutes, until the fillets turn golden brown. Serve with lemon slices, vegetables in season, or a salad of your choice.

Sea Catfish

LOCATION

Australia wide.

DESCRIPTION

The body of a catfish is not unlike a flathead, with the back of the fish running down to a very thin tail which is without the normal 'V'. The head is flat and there are two protruding whiskers.

Wear gloves when handling the catfish; their spines are highly poisonous.

BAIT

Whitebait, cockles (pipi), worms, small pieces of fish.

GEAR

As catfish are caught in shallow waters, a normal jetty rod like the Silstar 1100–90BWS and an EX2150 reel is ideal. The line should be about 6-kg breaking strain and a bottom rig of a 30-gram bean sinker above two number 4 beak hooks keeps the bait where the fish is, right on the bottom.

HOW TO CATCH

The best time to fish for catfish is at night. They frequent the shallow waters on estuaries and rivers, mainly close to sandbars. Many are speared with flounder. Do not worry too much about the depth of water, as the catfish will come into a few centimetres.

Cast well out on to the bar and slowly retrieve. The disturbed sand will attract the catfish. They have a big mouth, so strike hard when they bite to sink the hook firmly.

Have a sharp knife handy and when the fish is beached, cut the head off straight away. By doing this the fish is

allowed to bleed properly, leaving a clean, white flesh. Skin the fish from the neck down.

HOW TO COOK

Boil a Sea Catfish until the flesh is white and easily flaked. Flake the fish until you have about 1 kg. Mix the fish with about 600 ml of curry sauce. Reheat the mixture thoroughly in the oven. Serve with celery and creamed potatoes, or rice and diced carrots.

Murray
Cod

LOCATION

River Murray, Darling River, and their tributaries.

DESCRIPTION

Silver to deep green back, big head and mouth, and a broad, fat tail.

BAIT

Yabbies, freshwater shrimp, rabbit flesh, River Murray oysters, small fish like Boney Bream, and floppy lures. However, the natural baits are best.

GEAR

Rods can range from the Silstar 1280 70BWS with an EX2170 reel to big surf rods for casting deep offbank holes. The line should be about 10-kg breaking strain fitted with a 60-gram pyramid sinker and two 4/0 beak hooks.

HOW TO CATCH

The Murray Cod is the old man of the river system and likes nothing better than to lie in deep holes under the cliffs during the day, waiting for food to come to him. A cod could spend most of its life in one area. However, at night it moves from its deep hideaway on to the mudflats in search of small fish and yabbies. These flats are always on the inside of the turn in the river where the water travels slower in floodtime. Cast your line well out from the bank, so that the bait lies on the edge of these mudbanks. From a boat you can test where the bank starts with a simple leadline over the side. These areas are worth fishing until an hour after sun-up, and then you should move to the deeper water.

When using live yabbies, simply set the hook through the tail. This will keep the yabby alive and attractive to

the fish. When using Boney Bream, set the hook high in the back of the fish near the neck, being careful not to harm the lateral line. Let them swim freely around with loose line. You could get snagged occasionally, but the end result is worth this inconvenience.

Set the drag well below the breaking strain of the line, as the Murray Cod is a very powerful fish. It will swim strongly when hooked, without much of the fight of fish like salmon or barramundi, but its sheer power is enough to break a line. Use a gaff to beach the fish.

When cleaning the catch, remember that the cod has a heavy lining of fat around the backbone and this must be removed before putting the fish into the pan.

HOW TO COOK

Lay Murray Cod cutlets on an oven-proof dish and season with salt, pepper, basil, and bay leaves. The oven temperature should be about 200°C. Dice spring onions finely and place them around the fish in the dish. Add half a cup of cooking oil, a cup of white wine, and about 60 grams of butter. Bake for about 25 minutes. Garnish with parsley and serve.

Rock
Cod

LOCATION

Australia wide.

DESCRIPTION

Rock cod come in a variety of colours, with a small head on a large body. Not unlike a small groper.

BAIT

Fish flesh, cockles (pipi), squid.

GEAR

From the shore a surf rod like the Silstar 999–100BWS with an ST2070 reel is ideal, and from a boat the Silstar 1100–76BWB fitted with an EX2150 reel is best. A conventional two number 3 limerick hooks above a 60-gram pyramid sinker is best. If the shore angler is fishing among rocks, and he probably will be, use the two hooks on a 1-metre trace below a bob float.

HOW TO CATCH

There are numerous species of rock cod and, in most cases, they are despised by anglers. They look ugly and their flesh is thick and oily. Despite this they make fine eating on the barbecue. They can be found near any rocky shore. When fishing for rock cod, always wear gloves, as they have a thick spine on the back and very sharp teeth. If you are fishing from rocks, take extreme care. Check the fishing spot carefully. If the rock is wet, stay away from it, for this means that a wave has broken over it recently. There is no such thing as a freak wave. One in about every seven is much bigger than the rest, and this is the wave to watch.

Always keep moving the line when fishing for rock cod. They have a very sharp bite and should be struck immediately this is felt. Otherwise, the bait will be right

down their throat and hard to get out. This is where the gloves come in. It is also advisable to use a wire trace, as their teeth will fray nylon line in a few minutes.

They should be killed and gutted immediately, as their stomach lets off an odour which will permeate the flesh if left too long. An excellent sport fish which put up a good fight, their size makes them fun to catch.

In most cases an 8-kg line is ideal, but if you want some real sport try catching them on line as light as 3 kg. However, do not forget the landing net. The biggest and best rock cod are generally found in sheltered rocky areas, which makes it ideal for shore and boat fishing.

HOW TO COOK

Oily fish like the rock cod are ideal on the barbecue. Place fillets on a very hot plate and continually sprinkle with a white wine.

Turn each fillet every two minutes until cooked. This is a simple recipe which can be used at most times near the fishing spot where cod are plentiful. Eat the fillets between two slices of fresh buttered bread.

Crabs (Blue)

LOCATION

Blue Sand Crabs—Queensland and northern New South Wales; Blue Swimmers—South Australia and Western Australia.

DESCRIPTION

The male crabs are a rich blue and the females brown. The Swimmer has big main claws.

BAIT

Fish, squid, or red meat.

GEAR

Drop or cone nets, or dab nets and rakes.

HOW TO CATCH

There is nothing like a day's crabbing with the family. From a boat, drop and cone nets are used. The drop net is about 80 cm across and lies flat on the bottom with the bait in the centre, and the cone net has the rim of the net on the bottom with the net rising from it and the bait in the centre. The cone net tangles the crab in the net; the drop net is pulled so that the crabs fall into the net. I prefer the drop net.

Old fish heads make ideal bait. However, these must be replaced or added to every 15 minutes so that the smell remains in the water. The crabs are guided to the bait by the smell, so always crab on a fairly fast-flowing tide. Never use the heads of a crab predator in the nets—such as snapper and mulloway (jewfish). Whiting, bream, garfish, and tommy ruff are good bait. Pull the nets every five minutes. This is long enough for a crab to find its way in.

Dabbing crabs can also be fun. The dabbing spots are long, shallow sand patches and light mudflats. This is

where the crabs bury in the sand. On calm days you will be able to see two small eyes sticking out of the sand, with a slightly disturbed patch of sand where the body is hidden. Rub the dab net or rake along the sand. When it strikes a crab, it will come out of the sand immediately into a defensive attitude, claws up. At this point they are simple to dab.

The best time to dab is as the tide is falling, when the crabs will be swimming to deeper water.

HOW TO COOK

Boil the Blue Swimmer or Sand Crabs in saltwater, or sea water if it is available. If tap water has to be used, add a cup of common salt to each medium-sized pot. Let them boil for five minutes and then cool them quickly under a running tap to set the meat. Remove the back shell, but do not throw it away. Clean the gut including the 'feathers' from the top of the crab. Carefully replace the back shell and place it on a fish plate. Serve with tomatoes, lettuce, celery, and tartare sauce.

Crayfish

LOCATION

Victoria, South Australia, Tasmania, Western Australia.
There is also a green tropical crayfish, which will not
enter pots, in Queensland and the Northern Territory.

DESCRIPTION

Brown to a green-brown in colour when taken from the
water. They have a large spiny tail and two spiky horns
on the head, as well as two long feelers. Not to be confused
with lobsters, which have a similar body but with two
nipper claws. They are not found in our coastal waters.
However, there is a River Murray Lobster with nippers.

BAIT

Any fish or meat flesh.

GEAR

Crayfish pots with an entrance hole in the top, drop nets
similar to crab nets, or a line-and-bait method can be used
from the rocks.

HOW TO CATCH

The line-and-bait method is very effective. Here the bait
is placed in an old pair of pantyhose stockings and weight
is added to make it sink. This is then tied to a 20-metre
heavy cord line. It is then cast near the limestone rocks
jutting out into the sea. Crayfish like limestone to make
their homes more than any other rock.

When the line moves start steadily, but slowly, to pull it
in. The crayfish will pull back, but the backward facing
spikes on its body, tail, and legs will snag in the pantyhose just long enough for you to get a dab net under it.

Drop nets should be baited in the same way with meat
in pantyhose. Again this will prevent the crayfish scurry-

ing off when you start to pull the net. Next time you are
rock fishing, give this a try.

HOW TO COOK

To prepare crayfish, remove the tail from the shell and
cut into small pieces. Dice the white of a hard-boiled egg.
Put the crayfish and the egg into a saucepan with a stiff
white sauce and heat well. Remove the pan from the stove
and add lemon juice and a tablespoon full of cream. Fill
the shell from which you took the crayfish meat with the
mixture, and garnish with lemon and parsley.

Dart

LOCATION

All Australian states.

DESCRIPTION

The body is similar to a trevally but it has two dark spots. It has a long, slender swallow tail, and a fine upper and lower fin. The head is small.

BAIT

Whitebait, bluebait, cockles (pipi), worms, and well-crushed squid.

GEAR

Use a rod similar to the Silstar 1100–70SBM and an AT2550 sidecast reel. The line should be about 6-kg breaking strain with a single number 5 limerick hook. Do not use a sinker if at all possible. If weight has to be used, try a small piece of split shot.

HOW TO CATCH

The dart is found wherever there is a rocky outcrop associated with limestone. They feed mainly on oyster spat and small crustacea, including worms.

Dart are a timid fish, and the baits have to look completely natural—just a bait slowly sinking in the water or just laying on the bottom. The line should be kept loose so that when the fish takes the bait it feels no weight. If there is little or no tide running, try dropping small pieces of cockle (pipi) for berley.

Its biting action is much the same as the sweep. They pick the bait up, feel no weight, swallow and keep swimming. However, once hooked they put up a good fight by laying on their side and swimming in circles.

The mouth is relatively soft, so take care when boating

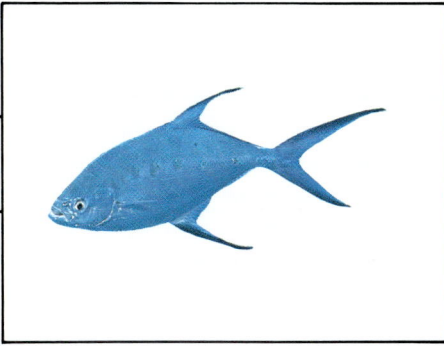

the fish. If it is over 500 grams use a landing net or you will risk losing the fish.

HOW TO COOK

Scale, clean, and head the dart. Coat each fish with butter and sprinkle with basil, pepper, salt, and parsley flakes. Sprinkle beer over each fish. Place the fish on double foil and wrap tightly. Cook on a preheated griller on the barbecue for about 10 minutes. Garnish with lemon and serve with salad.

Dhufish

LOCATION

Western Australia.

DESCRIPTION

Brown to silver on the back, small head, and big strong tail. It has a large mouth.

BAIT

Octopus, squid, pilchards, bluebait, and small mullet.

GEAR

Most of these fish are caught on reefs offshore in southern Western Australia. A Silstar 1100–66BWJ rod matched with the EX2150 reel is ideal. Breaking strain of lines vary with the size of the fish. They grow up to 30 kg. A good starting point for a line is about 8 kg. Being a reef fish, the hooks have to be kept well above the rocks. Fit a pyramid sinker about 40 cm below two 3/0 beak hooks. Give the hooks a good long trace, so they can float freely in the water.

HOW TO CATCH

Dhufish live on offshore reef areas. One of the most popular is off the south-west coast of Fremantle, near Rottnest Island. Hundreds of anglers fish this area each year in search of this fine table fish. It is classed as one of the best in Australia.

The dhufish is a good fighter and must be treated with respect. Use big baits, whole pilchards at a time. If the waters are shallow enough in the reef area, try using live mullet bait. For this you change the rig to a 60-gram sliding sinker above a 2-metre trace. This will allow the fish to swim freely on the bottom. Keep the rod in a holder or hold it all of the time, because when a dhufish

strikes it has tremendous power. Many a rod has gone overboard on the first run.

Set the drag on the reel carefully and once the initial fight is over, gradually increase it. Keep the tip of the rod up and let it take all of the sudden shocks.

Always use a landing net or gaff to boat the fish.

Unfortunately this fine sport and eating fish has been exploited over the years and their numbers are not what they used to be, so only catch what you can eat. Leave the rest for another day.

HOW TO COOK

Mix a traditional batter of self-raising flour, egg, and milk. Take cutlets of dhufish and roll them liberally in the batter. Heat a deep frypan of cooking oil to near boiling. When the temperature is right, the fillets should float on the oil. Cook until the batter colour changes to a golden brown. This should only take a few minutes. Serve with chips only and you have a genuine fish-shop special.

Red
Emperor

LOCATION
Tropical reefs in northern Australia.

DESCRIPTION
Pink in colour with darker bands around the body. A small head, deep body, and strong tail structure.

BAIT
Small fish, prawns, squid.

GEAR
Most Red Emperor are caught from a boat and therefore a top quality rod and reel is needed. Try the Silstar 1280 10JIG rod matched with an AX2670 reel spooled with 12-kg breaking strain line. Two 4/0 hooks.

HOW TO CATCH
The Red Emperor is generally caught in deep channels running through reef areas offshore. They grow up to 20 kg and put up a great fight.

Set the drag on the reel to about 5-kg breaking strain to begin with. Most of these fish are caught on the drift therefore a rig with a 90-gram pyramid sinker set about 50 cm below the two hooks is ideal. This will keep the hooks close enough to the bottom for the fish but well away from small outcrops of reef which can snag the line. The baits should be big and sloppy with only a small part of the point of the hook protruding.

When the fish is hooked get all other lines out of the water or you could be looking at a major tangle.

Keep the tip of the rod well up and gradually increase the drag as the fish tires. Strike hard when the fish first takes the bait as it has a big, hard mouth.

Use a gaff or landing net to boat the fish.

HOW TO COOK

A beer batter gives a delightful flavour to Red Emperor.
Use a cup of flour, salt, an egg, and beer. Mix until stiff.
Generally half a cup of beer will suffice. Let the mix stand
for about half an hour. Cover the fillets in seasoned flour
and dip them in the batter. Fry in hot butter for about two
minutes each side. Garnish with parsley and lime slices
and serve with a salad and slices of avocado.

Flathead

LOCATION

Queensland, New South Wales, Victoria, Tasmania, South Australia, and Western Australia.

DESCRIPTION

Large, spiny head with a slim, tapered body. Colour ranges from dark brown to grey and light brown. There are numerous species.

BAIT

Fish fillets, whitebait, bluebait, shrimp, prawns, pilchards, cockles (pipi), and squid.

GEAR

Use a firm but light-tipped rod like the Silstar 1282 66SP and an AX2650 sidecaster reel. The line should be about 6-kg breaking strain. Use a sliding rig, that is a 60-gram bean sinker set above two number 3 beak hooks on a 1-metre trace. This ensures the baits are on the bottom at all times.

HOW TO CATCH

The two major flathead species live in vastly different areas. One lives on the mud and sand flats of estuaries, and the other on reef areas offshore. However, they both have the same feeding habits. They live mainly on small fish and stay in the same areas for long periods of time. They are well hidden by their body colours and move slowly across the sea floor until the prey is sighted. Then they move surprisingly quickly. They have a big, hard mouth and two poisonous spines on either side of the gills, so it is wise to wear gloves when handling them.

The best way to catch flathead is from a boat on the drift. This drift should be slow, so that the fish have time to see the bait as it passes by. When a flathead is hooked,

drop a marker buoy so that you can return to the spot and drift from it again and again. Flathead vary in size from 250 grams to 10 kg, so be prepared for a fight if a big one takes the bait. Have a landing net handy, and keep the tip of the rod up.

Flathead are also caught in great numbers from the shore and for this you need a surf rod like the Silstar 1100–12BWM. Use the same rig as from the boat. Cast from the beach, and slowly retrieve for the best results.

The flathead has a very large mouth and therefore the baits should be big. When using fish fillets, shape the bait like a small fish and leave a 2-cm tail hanging from the hook.

When the fish takes the bait, strike hard, as the flathead has a very hard bony mouth. And don't forget to watch those spikes behind the gills.

HOW TO COOK

Place fillets of flathead on foil and place under a pre-warmed griller. The cooking time of the fish should be about five minutes. Finely grate some tasty cheese. Take the fish out from the griller just before they are cooked, and sprinkle the cheese over each fillet. Put the cheese-covered fish back under the griller until the cheese melts. Add sprigs of parsley and serve.

Flounder

LOCATION

Australia wide, several species.

DESCRIPTION

Colour ranges from deep green to dark brown. A flat, bottom feeder with its mouth on the side and eyes on the back of the body.

BAIT

Shrimp, prawns, cockles (pipi), or worms.

GEAR

The flounder is a bottom feeder and this means that the baits have to lay on the bottom. For a rod try the Silstar 1282 66SP and an AX2650 reel. This rod can be used from a boat or from the shore. The rig is a light, sliding sinker, about 30 grams, above two number 4 limerick hooks. The hooks should be set about 30 cm apart. A 4-kg breaking strain line would be ideal for the average fisherman.

HOW TO CATCH

In most cases, flounder are speared at night in shallow estuary waters. One of the prime spots in Australia is in South Australia's Coorong area. Here the water is only a few centimetres deep. All the spear fisherman needs is an underwater light hooked to a 12-volt battery in a dinghy and a three-pronged spear. The spear fisherman will see two tiny red eyes in the sand. Aim the spear just behind the eyes to avoid damaging the fish's flesh.

From a boat the best way to catch flounder is on the drift. Allow the boat to drift at about 1 knot. This can be done by allowing a light bag of sand, about 10 kg, to drift along the bottom on the tide or wind. The flounder will be found mainly on a sandy bottom, so there is little or no

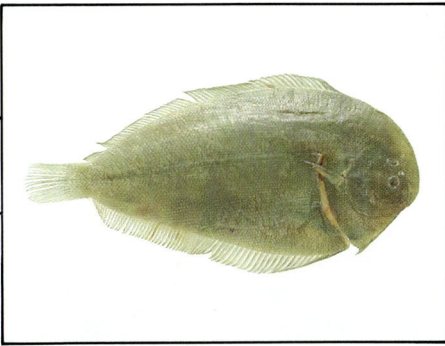

worry of lines getting snagged on the bottom. Always use big baits and wherever possible leave a tail hanging loose to help attract the fish.

In Tasmania many flounder are caught from bridges and banks, especially in the Derwent River area. Again a moving bait is best. Cast and slowly retrieve.

Flounder are also found in the mud areas which are normally fished by prawn trawlers. This is generally in deep water, but a drift over these areas is well worthwhile. Flounder look slow movers but they are surprisingly fast when they see a bait floating past. They naturally wait for food to come to them on the tide, but once they see it they can move in a flash.

Flounder is a fish which needs no filleting. It only has a main backbone and the meat is easily scraped free when cooked. The gut is small and there are few scales.

HOW TO COOK

Fried flounder makes a delicious meal. Allow one fish per person. Lace the stomach cavity with salt, pepper, and a shake of basil leaves. Heat the pan with butter and lemon juice to near boiling point. Coat the fish with seasoned flour. Place in the pan and cook it gently on either side. Serve on a heated dish and garnish with parsley and serve with French salad.

Garfish

LOCATION

Australia wide, in four species.

DESCRIPTION

Silver-blue to grey with a long, slender body and bill.

BAIT

Gents (maggots), cockle valve (pipi), clear fish flesh, worms, uncooked crayfish, or mince berley.

GEAR

From a jetty use a 3-metre rod similar to the Silstar 1100–86SPD and an EX2150 reel, and from a boat a Silstar 1280 60SP rod and an AX2640 sidecast reel. A floating rig is one of the best. From a jetty or wharf use a feed float about 30 cm behind a pencil float and a 1-metre trace. Fit two number 9 limerick hooks to the bottom of the trace. Some use three hooks but this only invites tangles when the fish are really biting. From a boat use no floats at all, only the two hooks. Another rig is a spring sinker fitted above the trace with a cork at the end of the trace. The two hooks lie between the cork and the sinker. This is very effective in shallow waters.

HOW TO CATCH

Garfish are, without doubt, the easiest fish in the sea to catch. They are scavengers but feed mainly on weed in inshore waters. They are brought to the surface with berley. This need not be too elaborate, just stale bread laced with a can of sardines (but be sure the sardines are in fish oil *not* vegetable oil). The berley stream should be heavy for about the first five minutes then reduced to just a trickle. If the garfish get too much berley they will go off the bite.

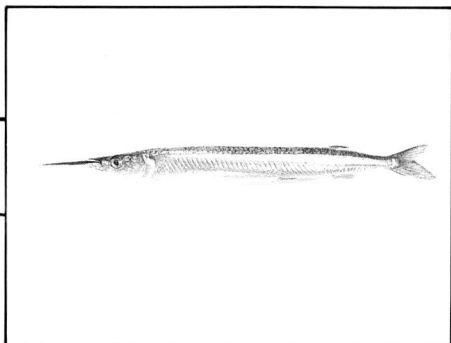

From the pier or jetty the feed float does the same job, but make sure the mixture is thick and sticky so that it does not flow from the float too rapidly. From a boat the garfish will come right up to the stern. However, these are not the fish you will catch. The hungry ones lie about 10 metres astern. Let the line out and leave it. The garfish will hook themselves.

All you have to do is pull them in. Often there will be a double header and when this happens leave the fish on the bottom hook until last when taking them off. This fish will hold the line tight while you take off the top fish.

Hold the fish by the head and slide the free hand down the body; this will remove all of the scales. This is called stripping and it saves a lot of time when you get ashore.

Always have a variety of baits on hand and change them regularly. Garfish have a habit of going off one bait very quickly but they will take to another type. Even then, change the baits regularly, as garfish rely on smell as much as anything.

Garfish schools will be found anywhere there is tape or posidonia weed. They are a summer fish in most cases, but many of the estuary species are caught in the winter months. They are a real beginner's fish and one of the finest eating in Australia.

HOW TO COOK

Take eight fillets of garfish for this delicious two-person meal. Bring water to the boil in a medium-sized saucepan. Place the fish on a plate and add two or three dobs of butter and a squeeze of lemon. Put the plate over the boiling water and place a lid over the fish. Test the fish after about 15 minutes. In most cases they are ready to eat. Large fillets take a little longer. Garnish fillets with parsley. Serve as an entree on its own or add a few chips, lettuce, and tomato to complete a full dish.

Groper

LOCATION

Australia wide, in a range of species.

DESCRIPTION

A small head and large mouth with a big thick body and flat thick tail. They range in colour from deep blue to grey and mottled.

BAIT

Any fish flesh and squid.

GEAR

From shore a stout surf rod like the Silstar 1100–66BWJ fitted with a big AT2570 sidecast reel is essential, and from a boat the Silstar and a similar reel is ideal. The line should be no less than 10-kg breaking strain and even heavier in the case of bigger fish. A simple pyramid sinker below two 6/0 hooks on wire traces is ideal. If a hand line is used, try a 40-kg breaking strain and a stout pair of gloves.

HOW TO CATCH

The groper inhabits caverns and caves in rocky outcrops along the shoreline and in deep water reefs. It is a territorial fish which rarely leaves home. It lets its food, small fish, come to it. Despite its size, it is remarkably fast when going after prey. Unfortunately, they are easy prey for unthinking spearfishermen and over the years have been slaughtered in thousands around Australia. Because of this, the Blue Groper is protected in South Australia.

From a boat, hunting the groper starts with an echo sounder. Look for steep drop-offs and start fishing on their edges. For bait use a whole squid or fish like a salmon or tommy ruff.

In most cases, groper do not bite like normal fish — they just swallow the bait and swim off. Strike hard when the line goes tight and be ready for a fight. If you land one groper in three strikes you will be doing very well. In most cases they head straight back to their cave and this makes it practically impossible for the fisherman to lift the fish. This is why heavy hand lines are often preferred to rods. The fisherman with the heavy hand line can lift the fish quickly as soon as it takes the bait, and get it away from its cave home.

Groper grow to the size of an average shark, way over the 80-kg mark. They are without doubt the old men of the sea and should be treated with respect.

There is no point in catching a boat load of them, only to see them wasted. Just catch what you want and then change to a light line for a bit of sport.

HOW TO COOK

Take cutlets of groper and coat them with seasoned flour. Heat butter, about two tablespoonsful, in a pan to near boiling. Cook the fillets in the pan for about one minute each side. Serve with slices of uncooked carrot, cheese, beans, and a few chipped potatoes. Do not overcook the fish or most of the flavour will remain in the pan. Garnish with parsley and orange slices.

Gurnard

LOCATION

Queensland, New South Wales, Victoria, Tasmania, South Australia, and Western Australia. Several look-alike varieties.

DESCRIPTION

Bright to deep red body with a big, spiny, ugly head and wafer-thin fins. The body is small in comparison with the head. Spiny, poisonous horns surround the head. Wear gloves when handling.

BAIT

Whitebait, squid, octopus, fish flesh, and prawns.

GEAR

A short stout rod with a fine tip like the Silstar 1100–56BWL and a mid-range EX2140 reel is the best. The line should be about 5-kg breaking strain. Gurnard feed on the bottom, therefore a sliding rig, similar to whiting, is necessary. Use a 60-gram bean sinker between two number 4 limerick hooks. Allow the sinker to slide about 40 cm.

HOW TO CATCH

The gurnard is a deep-water fish. They are caught in trawl nets near the continental shelf. However, deep-water areas like Port Fairy and Portland in Victoria and Port Lincoln in South Australia are well within the reach of these good eating fish. Do not be put off by the look of the fish; the flesh is white and tasty.

Most gurnard are caught on the drift. To do this the boat should be drifting at no more than half a knot. If it is moving too fast try using a bag with about 10 kg of sand as a drift anchor. The gurnard has a fast bite and, because of its big mouth, takes a bait right down easily. They range in size from 1 kg upwards, so be sure the drag on the reel

is correctly set. From the same patch you could get a 2 kg fish and a 5 kg fish.

Use a landing net to bring them aboard, and keep them well away from bare feet. A prick from the spines is unlikely to kill, but it can put paid to a day's fishing very quickly. Use an echo sounder to find the reef areas, but do not overlook areas where prawn trawlers are working. Gurnard are often on these flats in search of prawns.

HOW TO COOK

Boil a gurnard until the flesh comes away from the bone easily. Dice the flesh. Add a mixture of chopped onion, chopped parsley, a beaten egg, dices of celery, and finely grated cheese. Mix the fish and the ingredients into a smooth paste. Place in a square baking dish and tightly pack down. Put foil over the top. Bake in a 200°C oven for about 25 minutes. Remove the foil and bake for a further few minutes until the top goes a golden brown. This dish can be eaten hot with vegetables or cut and served cold as a fish loaf.

Hussar

LOCATION

Queensland, northern New South Wales, parts of the Northern Territory, and northern Western Australia.

DESCRIPTION

The body of the hussar is not unlike a snapper, but the head drops to a sharp point at the mouth. The mouth is big and strong.

BAIT

Cockles (pipi), prawns, shrimp, whitebait, squid, well-crushed and chunky fish pieces.

GEAR

Use a Silstar 1280 10JIG rod or similar fitted with a medium-range casting reel. The line should be about 10-kg breaking strain and the hook should be 2/0 beak. Fix two hooks on 20-cm traces above a 60-gram pyramid sinker. The sinker weight can be increased or decreased depending on the tide.

HOW TO CATCH

The Yellow-banded Hussar is a reef dweller which likes nothing more than to lie in a small cave and wait for small fish to swim past. It strikes like lightning. Therefore the angler should be looking for very rocky reef areas with big drop-offs. Drift over these areas, so that the bait you are offering looks natural to the fish.

At the first sign of a strike, hit hard and lift so that, while the fish is off guard, it is lifted away from its cave or hiding place. If the fish gets to the hole you may as well cut the line, because you will never get it out.

Be well prepared for a fight which could last up to half an hour, depending on the size of the fish. Take your time and get the fish. Use a gaff when boating the fish.

HOW TO COOK

Fry the fillets of the hussar in a frypan laced with butter. While it is cooking prepare a curry sauce. When the fish is cooked, chop it into mouth-sized chunks, add the curry sauce, and reheat. Serve with boiled potato, boiled whole beetroot, carrots, and silver beet.

John Dory

LOCATION

Queensland, New South Wales, Victoria, Tasmania, South Australia, and Western Australia.

DESCRIPTION

The John Dory is a deep bodied fish with a large head and a distinctive silver, circular patch in the centre of the body.

BAIT

Worms, cockles (pipi), shrimp, and squid.

GEAR

Use a rod similar to the Silstar 1280 66SP and an AX2650 sidecast reel. Set the trace with a pyramid sinker below two number 2 beak hooks.

HOW TO CATCH

John Dory are generally located in sand holes among offshore reefs and near wrecks. Their food source here is mainly small shrimp and worms. Many are caught annually in trawl nets.

They have a distinctly sharp bite and are known bait stealers. The angler must react very quickly to a bite or the bait is gone. Hold the rod all the time. Keep the bait moving with a slow lift and drop action. This will attract the fish to the baits.

The boat is generally anchored over the sand spot when fishing for John Dory, but a slow drift now and again can produce good results.

The John Dory has a fine eating flesh, but it should be kept cool at all times to avoid softening.

HOW TO COOK

Baked whole John Dory is easy to prepare. Place the whole fish in a baking dish with about a quarter of a cup of cooking oil and two cups of tomato juice.

Place it in a hot oven, about 200°C for about 30 minutes. Serve with mashed potato, parsley pieces, beans, and carrots.

Black
Kingfish

LOCATION

The Northern Territory, Queensland, northern New South Wales, and north-west Western Australia.

DESCRIPTION

Dark grey to black in colour with a large, strong tail and an extended lip on the lower jaw. The body shape is not unlike the Spanish mackerel.

BAIT

Whole fish like small mullet, salmon trout, tommy ruffs, and tailor. Heavy silver lures can also be used successfully.

GEAR

A Silstar light game rod fitted with a good-quality casting reel. The line should be about 12-kg breaking strain fitted with close snooded 5/0 beak hooks on a heavy nylon trace.

HOW TO CATCH

These fish are caught by trolling and often hooked when anglers are looking for tuna. They strike at great speed. The baits should be about 30 metres behind the boat and the line slightly weighted with two medium-size barrel sinkers, so that the bait remains just under the surface. The bait fish should be carefully hooked to the line so that it runs naturally in the water. Tie the nose of the fish to the line.

The Black Kingfish is a game fighter and skill is needed to bring it to boat. Set the drag well below the line's breaking strain. Sink the hooks well after a strike and let the fish run with a steady drag. Be sure there is at least 300 metres of line on the spool. The first run could take half of this.

Always use a gaff when boating the fish. Very little is known about the migration habits of the Black Kingfish, so be prepared all the time when you are trolling in northern waters.

HOW TO COOK

Roll large fillets of Black Kingfish in seasoned flour. Each fillet should be cut to the pan size. Heat oil in the pan. Place fillets in the pan and add one finely chopped onion and sprinkle the fillets with parsley. Cook for about 10 minutes. Just before the fish is fully cooked, sprinkle grated cheese over each fillet. Cook until the cheese melts. Serve with mashed potato, peas, and butternut.

Yellowtail
Kingfish

LOCATION

Queensland, New South Wales, Victoria, northern Tasmania, South Australia, and Western Australia.

DESCRIPTION

Similar in looks to a tuna, but more silver in colour with a yellow stripe and tail.

BAIT

Squid, pilchards, salmon trout, garfish, and whitebait.

GEAR

From the beach use a surf rod similar to the Silstar 1200 120BWM and an AT2590 sidecast reel. From a boat try the Silstar 1280 10JIG rod and an AX2660 similar reel. The line should be about 10 to 12-kg breaking strain. In most cases a drift rig with ganged number 3/0 limerick hooks is ideal. If weight has to be added, use a 30 to 60-gram bean sinker set about 1 metre above the hooks. If fishing near a rocky bottom, use a bob float about 1 metre from the hooks.

HOW TO CATCH

Yellowtail Kingfish can be found on many shorelines, near rock outcrops, under piers and jetties, and off break-waters. In the southern states the best time to fish them is in the summer months. In the water they look a lazy fish, but do not be fooled. They are real fighters with power close to that of the tuna.

They are a very wary fish which seem to sense danger quickly. I have seen them feed off fish scraps from a pier, almost in a frenzy, but when a hook was placed with the offal, they shied away. In many cases they have to be tricked into biting.

One of the best ways to catch the kingfish is with live squid, their favourite meal. Set the hooks gently in the underbelly of the squid and let it swim away with a loose line without sinkers. The squid will eject ink and this will attract the kingfish. Leave plenty of loose line as the fish will take several bites at the squid before it has all been taken.

Be sure the drag on the reel is set well below the breaking strain, because once the fish feels the weight of the line it will be off like a shot. These big fish can weigh in at about 40 kg. Keep the tip of the rod up and let it do the work. Take your time reeling it in. At times it can take half an hour to get a big fellow to gaff.

Kingfish can also be caught when drifting and casting. Here a whole garfish or small Striped Mackerel is ideal bait on the ganged hooks. Set the hooks as close as possible to the head of the fish, with the nose of the fish tied to the line so that it looks natural in the water.

The Yellowtail Kingfish is a real sports fish where skill and patience is the keynote.

HOW TO COOK

Take four Yellowtail Kingfish cutlets and lay them in a baking dish. Around the cutlets add whole tomatoes, slices of red peppers, and mushrooms. The oven should be about 180°C. This dish should take about 40 minutes to cook. However, check after 25 minutes and then every five minutes. When it comes out of the oven, squeeze a lemon over the fish and garnish with parsley. Serve with boiled potatoes.

Leatherjacket

LOCATION

Reef areas around Australia.

DESCRIPTION

The leatherjacket is the ugly fish of the sea. It ranges in a variety of colours from deep silver and blue to brown and yellow and much more. It has a short head with big grinding teeth, and a sharp spine on the top of the back.

BAIT

The leatherjacket will take practically any kind of bait, from fish flesh to squid, cuttlefish, shrimp, worms, and many more. However, its favourites are cockles (pipi) and crushed squid.

GEAR

From rocks use a Silstar 1100–120BWH surf rod and an EX2170 reel and from a boat use a Silstar 1100–66SP rod with an EX2150 reel. The line should be about 5-kg breaking strain with two number 5 long shank limerick hooks. Use wire traces to the hooks. Set the hooks above a 60-gram pyramid sinker.

HOW TO CATCH

Found on all reef areas around the coast, the thing to remember about leatherjackets is that they are lazy feeders. They do not run with a bait, swim off with it, or anything else. They will just lie next to it and nibble away. At times the angler will feel nothing on the line; at most it will be a faint pick. Therefore it is important to keep jagging the line about every five seconds.

Another method of catching leatherjackets is to use jag-type hooks on the line. That is, three hooks joined to a single eye. Bait these hooks with the points and barbs exposed and keep jagging. You will hook the leather-

jackets in the mouth, the back, the tail, and all over the place, but you will get the fish.

Do not be put off by their appearance; they make fine eating. It is important to clean the leatherjackets as you catch them. This only take a few seconds. Cut through the backbone from the top of the back just behind the spine and tear the head free from the body. All of the gut will come with it. Then peel off the skin from the neck to the tail, and the fish is ready for the pan. The soft skin leatherjacket makes the best eating. The reason this must be done immediately is that the leatherjacket's stomach is very smelly and this permeates the flesh as the fish dies. It may not be the best looking fish in the sea, but do not waste it; it makes fine eating.

HOW TO COOK

Mock Crab is made by skinning and gutting a leatherjacket. Boil the fish with Blue Swimmer Crabs or Sand Crabs for about five minutes. This can be done while the crab catch is cooking. Leave the leatherjackets in the boiling water for a further five minutes to make sure the flesh is completely soft. Scrape the flesh from the body and mix with a small amount of crab meat. None of your friends will tell the difference.

Lingfish

LOCATION

All states.

DESCRIPTION

Generally red to pink in colour. It has a small head, not unlike a catfish, a thick body with fine fins the full length top and bottom, and a small tail. The skin has a slimy feel about it.

BAIT

Cockles (pipi), worms, and whitebait.

GEAR

Lingfish prefer inshore reef areas to feed and this puts them within the reach of the boat fisherman. A shore boat rod like the Silstar 1280 66SP and an AX2650 sidecast reel should do the job. The line should be about 8-kg breaking strain and the rig is a sliding sinker between two number 3 beak hooks. The sinker should be allowed to travel about 40 cm. Use big baits.

HOW TO CATCH

The lingfish is a bottom feeder and a relatively slow mover. It hunts its food in the same manner as a flathead. It gives a weak bite and this is because it likes to chew at a bait rather than swim off with it. Make the baits big and sloppy.

Lingfish grow to several kilograms in weight and put up a good fight when hooked. Use a landing net.

Do not be put off by their appearance. They have a thick white flesh and it is full of flavour. It should be skinned, not scaled. Lingfish is a big market fish in Eastern state markets.

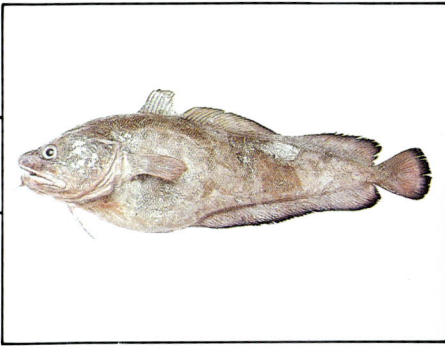

HOW TO COOK

Take fillets of lingfish and lay them flat on a work bench. Cut a pocket in each fillet. Put champignon caps, chopped shallots, a touch of crushed garlic, and some crab meat in each fillet. Roll the fillets with all the ingredients tucked inside. Secure the fillets with a tooth pick. Place them in a baking dish and pour white wine over them. Cook for about 30 minutes in a 200°C oven.

Blue
Mackerel

LOCATION

Eastern seaboard, Victoria, South Australia, and southern Western Australia.

DESCRIPTION

A slender, big, thick body, light blue in colour with darker blue stripes down each side. It has big eyes and a fine powerful tail.

BAIT

Fish pieces, cockles (pipi), pilchard, whitebait, and squid.

GEAR

A light jetty rod like the Silstar 1100–66SP and an ST2050 reel is best for shore fishermen, and from a boat a shorter Silstar is best. In both cases the rod should be light on the tip and firm at the butt. I find a floating rig best when at anchor or a conventional snook (pike) rig while trolling. The floating rig is two number 4 limerick hooks weighted with a small piece of lead shot, just enough to get the line a few metres under the water.

HOW TO CATCH

Mackerel are furious feeders. They will snap at anything moving in the water. They are not one of the greatest table fish, as their flesh goes soft very quickly after they are caught, but they put up a great fight on light gear. Try using a 3-kg breaking strain line for real sport.

Let the line drift out from the back of the boat in a berley stream. The berley should contain sardines in fish oil, fish pieces, and bread. This will hold the fish at the back of the boat. If you are using light gear, be careful as you retrieve the line. Mackerel tend to lie on their side when on the run and keep a steady strain on the line.

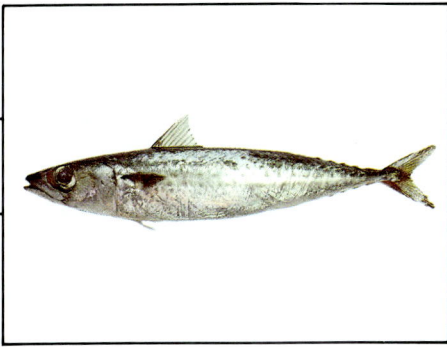

They will dart about all around the back of the boat. Other lines should be kept clear.

Cut their throats as soon as they come aboard, as they are a blood fish.

By the way, mackerel make ideal bait for snapper and snook. They can be frozen for later use, but if you do want them for bait do not bleed them. The blood is part of the attraction to a snapper.

HOW TO COOK

To prepare barbecued whole mackerel, roll the fish in wholemeal flour. Place it on a hot, well-greased barbecue. Continually turn the fish to avoid sticking. It will take about five minutes. Serve with a few slices of potato and onion.

Horse
Mackerel

LOCATION

Victoria, South Australia, and parts of Western Australia.

DESCRIPTION

Silver-yellow in colour with a smooth skinned body, big eyes, and short spines on either side of the tail. Also known as chow or scad.

BAIT

Whitebait, worms, fish flesh, and squid.

GEAR

A 3-metre jetty rod like the Silstar 1100–66SP and an ST2040 reel is ideal. Use a 4-kg breaking strain line. Two rigs can be used. The bottom rig is a spring, berley sinker (about 30 grams), below two number 7 limerick hooks. The other is a drift line with a bob float and the two hooks about 1 metre below it.

HOW TO CATCH

Horse Mackerel generally swim in schools near reef outcrops or over broken limestone bottom. In the southern states they arrive in thousands during the summer months. They are not a good eating fish, but they can provide good sport for fishermen.

They are brought around a boat with a berley stream similar to garfish and tommy ruff. However, they rarely bite on a fast-flowing tide. As the tide stops and the berley sinks deeper in the water, the Horse Mackerel rise from the bottom.

They have a very quick bite, so the angler has to strike as soon as he feels the slightest tug on the line. Wear a light pair of gloves, as the back spines on the tail can irritate the back of the hand.

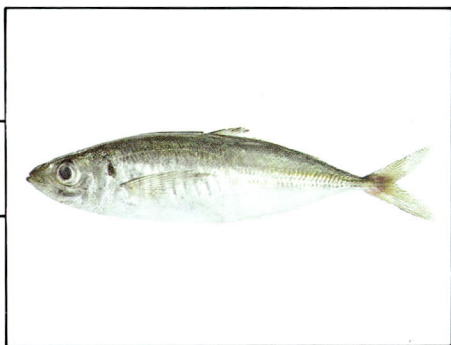

Horse Mackerel generally school in the same areas as snapper abound, and this makes them an ideal bait.

HOW TO COOK

About 500 grams of cooked Horse Mackerel can make a delicious meal. First shred the fish, add two eggs, parsley, and half a cup of milk. Melt butter in a pan and pour in the mix. Stir until the mix becomes creamy. Serve on toast.

Spanish
Mackerel

LOCATION

Queensland, Northern Territory, northern New South Wales, and northern Western Australia.

DESCRIPTION

Slender, powerful body with a fine tail and small head. Its colour is green-blue on the back to white on the underbelly.

BAIT

Small fish, and octopus and squid strip bait.

GEAR

A semi-game rod is best, like the Silstar 1280 10GAM with full roller runners. A heavy, top of the range AX2670 reel is also needed to handle these fast-running fighting fish.

HOW TO CATCH

Spanish Mackerel are caught by trolling behind a boat in most cases, though they have often been caught by rock fishermen. However, fishing from the rocks for these big fish is a job for an expert angler.

From a boat, a bait or lure is trolled behind the boat at about 5 knots. The line is about 20-kg breaking strain, fitted to a wire trace. A whole small fish like a chow or big garfish is used for bait. Strips 15 cm by 3 cm of squid or octopus can also be used to attract the big ones.

The new Comstock cable bait hook is ideal for setting a hook in whole fish. With this the fisherman threads the wire cable through the anus of the fish and back through the body and mouth. This leaves the hook exposed under the fish and the fish trolls naturally in the water. Ganged 6/0 limerick hooks can also be placed through the side of the fish with a light piece of cord holding the trace to the nose of the fish so that it lies right in the water.

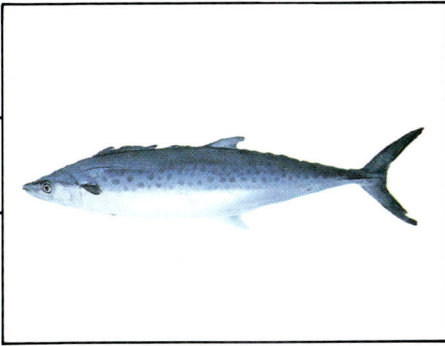

When fishing for Spanish Mackerel the rod should be held all the time or placed in a firm holder. Never leave it resting on the boat.

The reel should be set with a loose drag so that when the fish takes the bait, and it does at tremendous speed, it can run. Sink the hooks and keep the rod up so that its full action is working. Increase the drag as the fish tires. You can retrieve some of the line by 'pumping' the rod, that is, pulling it back and winding quickly as you drop the tip. However, do not do this with a jerking action or you risk losing the fish. Keep winding all of the time so as to keep pressure on the fish and reel in line. Gaff the fish when it comes alongside.

HOW TO COOK

Coat fillets or cutlets of Spanish Mackerel with seasoned flour. Heat a pan, with butter and a few cloves of garlic. Place the fish in the pan and sprinkle parsley flakes over each side of the fillet as it is cooking. This should take about two minutes each side. Serve with a French salad. Garnish with parsley and lemon slices.

Blue
Morwong

LOCATION

Victoria, South Australia, and Tasmania.

DESCRIPTION

The Blue Morwong has a sleek, thick body like a trevally. Its head is small and it has a powerful, fine tail. Its back is a deep blue running into silver, with a few yellow spots.

BAIT

Worms, pilchards, whitebait, cockles (pipi), and prawns.

GEAR

Most Blue Morwong are caught from boats, and this makes the new-style Silstar 1280 70BWC an ideal rod. This rod matched with an AT2570 sidecast reel is ideal. The line should be about 8-kg breaking strain. I find a drift rig of two 1/0 beak hooks ideal. Add just enough lead shot to get the line near the bottom.

HOW TO CATCH

The Blue Morwong is a reef dweller and a very wary fish. It will inspect a bait thoroughly before striking. This is why the hooks have to be completely covered with bait, but be sure the point is not snagged with a hard piece of flesh. This fish has a small, hard mouth and likes to suck at a bait. Its final bite is hardly stronger than a garfish pick.

I find drifting over the reef area the best, as the fish do not school but hunt for food on their own. When the fish takes the bait, strike hard to bed the hook firmly into the mouth. And be prepared for a fight. The Blue Morwong is a very powerful fighter and will not give up easily. They will fight longer and harder than a snapper. Start with a light drag, and increase the drag as the fish tires.

When the fish is played out it will lie on its side like a snapper. Use a landing net or gaff to boat the fish.

The best time for Blue Morwong fishing is in the cold winter months.

HOW TO COOK

Select thick fillets of Blue Morwong, enough for the family. Insert foil in a big pan and half fill with a port wine. Bring the wine to the boil and place the fillets into the wine. Boil for about five minutes. The wine will give a delightful flavour to the fish. Garnish with parsley and orange slices and serve with carrots, beans, and mashed potatoes.

Dusky
Morwong

LOCATION

South Australia, Victoria, and southern Western Australia.

DESCRIPTION

Long, heavy mottled brown body with a small head and mouth. Also known as strongfish.

BAIT

Worms and cockles (pipi).

GEAR

A stout surf rod such as the Silstar 999–100BWS and a ST2070 sidecast reel. The line should be about 8-kg breaking strain and the best rig is a 60-gram bean sinker above a 1-metre trace. Use two number 4 beak hooks.

HOW TO CATCH

This slow-moving reef dweller was nearly wiped out in the early 1970s by spearfishermen. It is a curious fish and an easy target for the spear. It feeds on small crustacea, worms, small shrimp, and the like.

Fish near the edge of a reef and allow the line to lie still on the bottom. This is a fish which has to find the bait, and even then there is no guarantee it will take it. Its mouth is small and hard and when it does strike the angler has to strike back hard.

These fish are often caught on limestone reefs when fishing for King George Whiting. They are a good fighter but their flesh is of poor quality.

HOW TO COOK

Boil a Dusky Morwong until the flesh whitens and flakes easily. Flake the fish finely and allow to cool. Mash an equal quantity of potatoes. Mix the fish and the potatoes with some fine chopped parsley, lemon juice, and salt. Prepare a mix of seasoned flour, egg, milk, and bread-crumbs. Pat the fish and potato mix into shapes and roll in the flour, then the beaten egg and milk, and finally the breadcrumbs. Deep fry in hot oil until they go a golden brown. They can be eaten hot or cold.

Red
Mullet

LOCATION

Worldwide in a large range of species.

DESCRIPTION

In most cases this fish is bright red in colour and in others there is a trace of yellow. As the fish dies it loses its colour gradually. It has a medium-sized sloped head with two whiskers under the lower jaw, hence the alternative name goatfish.

BAIT

Sea worms and cockles (pipi) are best, but shrimp and crushed squid can be used.

GEAR

Use a light jetty rod similar to the Silstar 999–100BWS from piers, jetties, and wharves, and a Silstar 999–56BWB from a boat. An ST2050 reel is ideal in both cases. The line should be about 5-kg breaking strain and the rig is similar to whiting, as the Red Mullet is a bottom feeder, Use a 30-gram bean sinker between two number 5 limerick hooks. The sinker should be allowed to run about 40 cm.

HOW TO CATCH

Start looking for Red Mullet on inshore reef areas and along the weed-line where the sea floor is slightly muddy. This is where the Red Mullet seeks out its worms and small sea creatures.

When baiting up, cover the hook completely, making sure the point is not snagged, and when using worms leave a tail hanging below the hook. Lift the line at regular intervals so that the fish can get a good look at the baits. Red Mullet have a very quick bite, so be on the alert. Strike at the first sign of the bite. When the Red Mullet sights its prey it moves in very quickly, grabs the

bait firmly, and swims off with it in its mouth. If you do not strike quickly, the fish will feel the weight of the line and sinker and drop the bait immediately. Red Mullet can be caught at any time of the day, for they are always hunting for food.

Until a few years ago they were used only for bait, especially for snapper. However, European migrants saw them as their own national fish and they became popular on the dinner table. They have a firm flesh when fresh, but go soft very quickly. Keep the catch in a cool spot under a wet bag.

In the southern states, Red Mullet generally go hand in hand with King George Whiting.

HOW TO COOK

Take fillets of Red Mullet and cook them quickly in well-heated butter. The fillets should only take three minutes to cook. Before taking them from the pan pour half a cup of pure orange juice over the fish. Allow this to just start boiling. Serve the fillets and pour the juice from the pan over the fish. Garnish with parsley.

Jumping
Mullet

LOCATION

Southern states of Australia.

DESCRIPTION

The Jumping Mullet has a small head with a dark eye. It is dark grey in colour and sports a thick, dark grey tail.

BAIT

Fine mince berley or a bread and dough mix.

GEAR

A 4-metre rod with a very fine tip, similar to the Silstar 1100–106BF, and a mid-range reel like the AT2550, is needed. The line should be no more than 2-kg breaking strain. Use a quill float which is weighted so that only the top 4 cm shows above the water. Fit a 2-metre trace with a single number 11 limerick hook snooded direct to the trace.

HOW TO CATCH

Jumping Mullet is, without doubt, the hardest fish in the sea for an amateur to catch. It has a small mouth and only sucks at a bait. They are found in seaside rivers, estuaries, and in most cases under wharves and piers.

They school in large numbers, making sheer frustration for the angler. They can see them, many weighing in over 2 kg, but they cannot catch them without a net. Big numbers are netted each year for the commercial market.

Here is how to go about catching Jumping Mullet. Squeeze a small amount of the mince berley or dough over the whole of the hook. The berley is a mixture of beef mince, crushed and minced a second time, flakes of old mouldy cheese; and finely broken bread crumbs. The dough is a mixture of flour, butter, and milk. This has to be a firm paste, so not too much milk.

Drop the baited hook into the school and let it sink to the quill float level. Do not move it in any way. Have your hand on the rod all the time. When the Jumping Mullet takes the bait, all you will see is the slightest movement on the float. It will bob about 1 cm or less in the water. When this happens lift the rod. Do not jag. It is a case of lift the fish in rather than wind in.

It is the most frustrating fishing you can find, but with practice you will come home with a good bag of this fine eating fish. Their flesh is firm and sweet, one of the best eating fish in the sea.

HOW TO COOK

Fish prepared the Japanese way can be tasty, especially on a hot day at sea. Cut thin fillets of fish from the back and tail of a Jumping Mullet or the like. These should be about 3 cm wide, 12 cm long, and 2·5 cm thick. Put the fillets on foil and place them in the hottest, sunniest part of the boat. Often this is just under the screen on the fly bridge. Leave them there for about two hours. In this time the sun has done the cooking. Add a dash of vinegar and a quick snack at sea is ready.

Yellow-eye
Mullet

LOCATION

Australia wide.

DESCRIPTION

Deep silver on the back with a white underbelly and a bright yellow eye.

BAIT

Sea worms, mince berley, cockles (pipi).

GEAR

The rod should be about 3 metres with a fine tip fitted with a light sidecast reel. The Silstar 1200–100BWS rod with an AX2660 reel is ideal. The line should be about 5-kg breaking strain. Use a 30-gram spring sinker below three number 9 limerick hooks. In some cases the sinker can be used above the hooks, generally on a sandy bottom where there is no need to snag the hooks.

HOW TO CATCH

The Yellow-eye Mullet is one of the most nutritious fish in the sea. It is a scavenger, hence the black stomach lining. It is found in practically every estuary or bay around Australia.

They are one of the easiest fish to catch. Worms are first class for bait but most prefer the mince berley. This is minced beef mixed with a can of sardines or semolina and stiffened with bread crumbs. The angler uses the berley in the spring sinker and the meat pieces on the hooks. The fish feeds on the berley from the sinker and finds the baited hooks at the same time.

These mullet give a very sharp bite and therefore it is essential that the fisherman holds the rod all of the time with a tight line. They like a moving bait. This means that the angler should cast and slowly retrieve all of the

time. However, it does not mean that he should go in for 'casting competitions' or his berley stream will get out of reach and the fish will go with it.

Another way of holding the fish close at hand is to put in a berley bag with the mince berley close to where you are fishing, so the stream goes past your line. The berley bag can be easily made from an old plastic bread bag with a few holes punched in it. (By the way, take the bag home with you; do not leave it on the bank after you have finished fishing.) Give the bag a shake every few minutes to ensure an even flow. When using a berley bag, a floating rig is often effective. That is, three number 9 hooks and no sinker. Let it flow out with the berley.

When fishing for mullet, it is essential that they are kept cool after they are caught. They have a very open type of flesh and go soft quickly in the heat of the day.

The best time to fish for mullet is on the rising high tide. They will be found scavenging in the shallowest water. They are an ideal fish for the beginner to catch and make a fine meal.

In deep estuaries a bob float can be used above the hooks. Allow about 1·5 metres of trace below the float. Mullet are one of the most prolific fish on the Australian seaboard. An average size mullet weighs in at about 500 grams but much bigger fish have been caught. The best time of year to fish is from March until May, but smaller numbers can be caught year round.

HOW TO COOK

Pan fry fillets of Yellow-eye Mullet without added batter or crumbs. This should take only a few minutes. In another pan boil a small quantity of white wine, about a cup full. Serve the fish fillets and pour the hot white wine over each fillet. Garnish with parsley and slices of lemon. This makes an ideal entree.

Mulloway

LOCATION

All states except the Northern Territory.

DESCRIPTION

A big silver fish with a broad fat tail, heavy scale, and large mouth. Also known as butterfish and jewfish.

BAIT

Small fish like garfish, tommy ruff, salmon trout, and pilchards, prawns, and cockles (pipi). Lures like the Mister Twister can be used but in my opinion there is nothing like natural bait.

GEAR

A Silstar 1100–120BWM rod for beach and rock fishing, or a 1280 70BWC for boats. A Silstar AX2670 sidecast reel is ideal. Use no more than 10-kg breaking strain line. Use a sliding sinker, about 60 gram or lighter, above a 1-metre trace of slightly heavier line than the main line. Snood two 3/0 beak hooks to the trace or gang three number 1 limerick hooks.

HOW TO CATCH

Mulloway are essentially an inshore fish that likes nothing better than pounding surf and quiet estuaries when hunting for food. It eats fish and shellfish. They are touchy at all times, and it takes real skill by the angler to catch them. Live bait is best, but they also like long, thin garfish fillets and whole bungum worms.

Mulloway are caught during the day, but they are essentially night feeders. Bait preparation is necessary for the best results. When using fillets, be sure that there is a long tail hanging from the hooks. When using live bait, place the second hook on the line through the top of the back of the fish, just below the gills. Be sure not to

harm the bait fish's lateral line or it will die quickly. Leave the bottom hook hanging over the fish's head.

When mulloway take a fish they always crush the head first, hence the second hook running free. Always leave plenty of loose line so that the mulloway can swim freely with the bait fish without feeling any weight from the angler.

When it runs, strike hard, as they have a very hard, bony mouth, and be ready for a fight. Mulloway run fiercely and often more than 100 metres of line can peel off before the first run is finished. Like the snapper, the mulloway will often 'play possum' and come in easily before a second run, which will be as fierce as the first. Be prepared for it and take your time. After the second run, start to tighten the drag on the reel but do not be too anxious. Always use a gaff or landing net.

The best places to look for mulloway, apart from the surf, are near breakwaters, bridges, or wrecks. When fishing for mulloway, it is essential that the rod be kept high or breakoffs will happen regularly. The rod has to take the shock of all of the fierce runs. Set the drag on the reel well below the breaking strain of the line initially and gradually increase it as the fish tires.

The best time to fish is on the change of tides at night, the darker the better. Like snapper, quietness is essential —no noise and no lights.

HOW TO COOK

Select thick fillets of mulloway and mix a batter of crushed cornflakes and egg. Roll the fillets in the batter until each has a thick coating. Bring butter in a pan to near boiling. Place the fillets in the pan for about three minutes each side or until the outside batter becomes a deep, golden brown. Serve with slices of banana, asparagus, and a few chipped potatoes.

Nannygai

LOCATION

Eastern coast of Australia, Victoria, Tasmania, South Australia, and parts of Western Australia.

DESCRIPTION

Bright orange to pink in colour with a body similar to a snapper, but the tail is more like a swallowtail. The mouth is big and the eyes large. Sometimes called Red Snapper.

BAIT

Worms, squid, cockles (pipi), prawns, and fish flesh such as pilchards and whitebait.

GEAR

From the shore a Silstar 1100–120BWM surf rod and a mid-range reel like the ST2070 is necessary. From a boat the Silstar 100–BWJ is ideal. The line should be about 8-kg breaking strain. Use a conventional rig: a 60-gram pyramid sinker below two 3/0 hooks. Keep the sinker about 50 cm from the hooks to avoid snagging on rocks. A 15-kg breaking strain hand line with a similar rig can also be used.

HOW TO CATCH

Nannygai live on heavy reef areas and are in constant movement. Like snapper, they are always being hunted by sharks. Use a berley made from old fish heads and backbones to hold the fish on the reef.

Their bite is similar to a snapper—pick, pick at first, and then a run. They are a hard fighter, so care with the reel drag should be taken.

If the nannygai are small, drop the hook size down to a number 1 beak. Use an echo sounder to find the reefs. The rougher the bottom, the better for nannygai.

They have good eating qualities, but keep them out of the sun or their flesh will go soft.

In most cases do not anchor the boat, just drift over the reef. Besides not losing an anchor, this is the best way to find the fish. As soon as one is hooked, drop a marker and drift back past it a number of times until the school moves on.

HOW TO COOK

Baked nannygai in tomato paste is a dish which appeals to many. Take a whole, cleaned fish and put in a baking dish. Add a small amount of cooking oil, about half a cup, and about 60 grams of butter. Add two cups of tomato paste (liquid); add water if needed. Bake for about 30 minutes in a 200°C oven. Add salt, pepper, and parsley to taste.

Parrot Fish

LOCATION

Rocky outcrops and reefs around Australia.

DESCRIPTION

They come in a multitude of colours, have a small head, similar to a rock cod, and a thick scale which is slightly slimy.

BAIT

Fish flesh, squid, cockles (pipi), red meat.

GEAR

From the shore use a surf rod similar to the Silstar 999–100BWS and an ST2050 reel. From a boat try the Silstar 999–56BWB rod and an ST2040 reel. From a boat the rig is a 60-gram pyramid sinker with two number 4 limerick hooks above. From the shore use a bob float with two similar hooks below; this is to avoid the rocks and weed along the shoreline. Use a wire trace.

HOW TO CATCH

Like the rock cod, the parrot fish is not a sought-after fish with amateur anglers. Hundreds are left to rot in the sun each weekend but this need not be if anglers knew their fine eating qualities. They have to be cleaned and scaled immediately for the best flavour to come out. They feed on only the best the sea has to offer—oysters, shrimp, cockles, small fish, and the like—and this is reflected in their flesh, which is white, clear, and firm.

The best place to look for parrot fish is in sheltered pools surrounded by rocks or coral. They have a lazy bite. Sometimes they give a sharp lick, and at other times they give no bite at all—simply swim past and swallow the bait. This means that the angler should be moving the bait constantly. As soon as any weight is felt, strike.

Always wear gloves as their back spine and teeth are sharp. Use about an 8-kg breaking strain line on the rods, and if you get a double header take the top fish off first to avoid tangles.

In most cases the parrot fish is classed as a beginner's fish on which a beginner can practice his fishing techniques. They are easily caught, but if you are fishing from rocks, take extreme care. Risking your life is not worth a few fish.

HOW TO COOK

Take fillets of parrot fish and marinate them in a red wine for about an hour. Dry the fillets and place them under a griller for about five minutes, depending on the size of the fish. Use greased foil under the fish to avoid sticking. Serve with a French salad and garnish with parsley and slices of lemon.

Red
Perch

LOCATION

New South Wales, Victoria, Tasmania, and southern South
Australia.

DESCRIPTION

A deep body with sharp fins towards the head, tapering
to fine fins near the tail. The tail is broad and fat and the
mouth is big with a large lower lip. There is a dark spot
on either side of the body towards the tail.

BAIT

Worms, cockles (pipi), oysters, small crabs, and well-
crushed squid.

GEAR

Use a Silstar 1100–120BWH with an AT2570 sidecast reel.
The line should be about 6-kg breaking strain fitted with
two number 1 beak hooks. As these fish are mainly caught
in deep water, a pyramid sinker should be used. This can
range from 30-grams upwards, depending on the tide
flow.

HOW TO CATCH

The red perch is found on rocky outcrops in water over
20 metres as a general rule.

It will take a well-prepared bait readily. Cover the
hook completely but be sure that the point of the hook is
not snagged. Remember, big baits catch big fish.

The red perch has a strong mouth, therefore once it is
hooked it is unlikely that it will break free unless the
fisherman puts too much strain on the line. However, it is
a good fighter, so care has to be taken after the first strike.
Try to get the fish away from the bottom, as it has a habit
of diving for the nearest rock or cave in the sea floor.

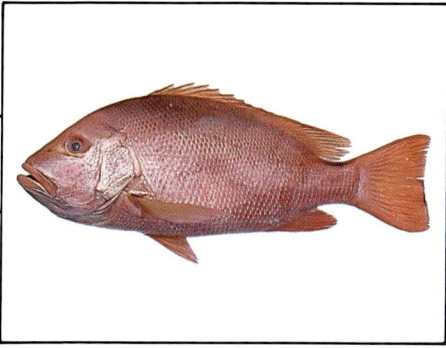

Always use a landing net or gaff when boating the fish. Keep it in a cool place on the boat, preferably on ice, as the flesh can go soft if heated.

HOW TO COOK

Take fillets of red perch and liberally cover each with butter. Place them on a well-greased grill. Cooking time will depend on the thickness of the fillets. Serve with grilled banana, curried rice, and baby carrots.

Redfin
Perch

LOCATION

Dams and streams in all states except the Northern Territory.

DESCRIPTION

Small head, deep body, with distinctive red fins.

BAIT

Tiger worms, freshwater shrimp, small yabbies, and lures like the Abu killer. The redfin will also take minnows.

GEAR

A light, whippy rod like the Silstar 1100–86SPD and an EX2150 reel is ideal. The line should be about 5-kg breaking strain. A light sinker, about 20 grams, can be used but in most cases a small bob float or a drift line is better.

HOW TO CATCH

Redfin perch are the fish scavengers of the river. They eat anything that moves, much like the salmon in the sea. Therefore it is important to keep the baits moving. For the best results, cast and retrieve continuously. However, if there is any wave action on the water, the bob float will have much the same result.

Keep moving from spot to spot, as redfin, like many other fish, have their favourite holes and these change as the food source dries up. When using lures, cast well along the banks and retrieve with a slow rhythmic action, so that you get the maximum work from the lure. Also try different depths when casting; let the lure sink further in the water every now and again.

Like the callop, the redfin likes nothing better than to hide near reeds and under trees, and then dart out as prey goes by. This is where you should be fishing. In the

case of the open dam, they will be nearer the centre where the water is cooler. This is where lures really come into their own. Major dams are also great spots for redfin, except in South Australia where such fishing is banned.

When a redfin is hooked in a tree-lined river, try to steer the fish away from the banks, as it has a habit of diving for the nearest tree root when hooked.

At times the flesh of the redfin can be rather bland. To overcome this rub rock salt into the fillets, leave them for five minutes, and then wash the salt out. This will give the flesh a real sea-fish flavour.

HOW TO COOK

Lemon-butter sauce gives great taste to fillets of redfin perch. Pulp a lemon and cut slices from the rind. Melt 30 grams of butter and add finely chopped parsley. Put the ingredients in a saucepan and add a few capers. Stir over a low flame until hot and then add the yolks of two beaten eggs, and stir. Return to the fire until it thickens but at no time let it boil. Pour the sauce over the cooked fillets. Top with sprigs of parsley.

Silver
Perch

LOCATION

New South Wales, South Australia, and Victoria.

DESCRIPTION

Small head with a large mouth. Deep silver on the back to light silver on the belly, with two sets of back spines.

BAIT

Worms, small yabbies, freshwater shrimp, and minnows.

GEAR

A 2-metre fine-tipped rod like the Silstar 1100–70SP and a mid-range EX2150 sidecaster reel. Use about a 4-kg breaking strain line fitted with a 1-metre trace and two number 4 limerick hooks. Add a small bob float about 2 metres above the hooks.

HOW TO CATCH

Silver perch like to lay in the shade of trees overhanging the river, preferably in deep holes. These holes are generally found on the widest bend of a river, where the water in floodtime travels faster than the shorter inside bank.

Cast the line about 2 metres out from the trees and let it drift back with the current. Do this two or three times and if there is no result try another bait. Always have a variety of baits with you. If there is still no result, try deepening the trace by about a metre. Keep moving from tree to tree if the fishing is slow.

If you are fishing the River Murray system, do not use worms or the only fish you will catch with them will be European Carp. Freshwater shrimp and minnows are the best bait in these waters.

Keep the catch cool all of the time or the flesh of the fish will go soft.

HOW TO COOK

Sousing is a good way to prepare silver perch. Put 300 ml of vinegar, bay leaves, salt, and six black peppers in a saucepan and boil for about five minutes. Put fillets of fish in a baking dish and strain the liquid over the fish. Place it in the oven and bake for about 30 minutes at 200°C. Allow to cool in the liquid and serve with a salad.

Queenfish

LOCATION

Northern Western Australia.

DESCRIPTION

The queenfish has the body of a tuna, right down to the serrated fins running down to the tail. It has a small head in comparison to the body and a large strong mouth.

BAIT

Have a range of heavy to light silver lures with heavy gauge hooks.

GEAR

A semi-game Silstar rod with a top quality casting reel. The line should be at least 12-kg breaking strain and for the best results use a mid-range silver lure with a heavy gauge number 3/0 limerick hook.

HOW TO CATCH

The queenfish likes reef areas where the waves break over a reef. Cast the lure where the white water meets the deeper green. Retrieve quickly, as this fish is accustomed to taking fast-moving fish and quick retrieval makes the lure look more lifelike. Halco makes a good selection of lures for this type of fishing.

They can be caught from a boat or the shore, depending on how far the reef is from the shore. Keep the rod at 45 degrees to the water all the time, and let the rod and reel work together.

Set the drag on the reel well below the breaking strain of the line, for when a queenfish strikes it takes off like an express train. It is, in my opinion, one of the best fighting fish in the sea. It will jump and 'walk' on the water to throw the lure, dive and make long runs, and test the angler to the utmost. By the way, queenfish have been

found in other northern states but Western Australia is their real home.

Do not try to gaff the fish until it lays on its side. If it is still upright in the water there is still plenty of fight left.

HOW TO COOK

The queenfish is delicious when cooked whole. They can be big fish, so this recipe can be used in the oven, Webber, or the barbecue. Season the fish with fresh breadcrumbs, thinly sliced onions or shallots, a chopped, peeled tomato, thin slices of celery, chopped spinach, chopped parsley, one egg, and salt and pepper to taste. Mix the seasoning and stitch into the fish's stomach with cotton or skewers. Lay the fish on double foil and add dobs of butter and slices of lemon. Wrap tightly. Cooking time should be about 30 minutes in a 200°C oven, and slightly longer on the barbecue. Serve with salads.

Salmon

LOCATION

Southern Australia.

DESCRIPTION

A heavy bodied fish with a small head and huge appetite. They are known as the sea vacuum cleaner, as they eat anything that moves when in a feeding frenzy. They are a green-grey in colour with yellow spots and a light yellow tail.

BAIT

Strips of any fish flesh, pilchards, whitebait, bluebait, or silver lures.

GEAR

From beaches a surf rod like the Silstar 1200–100BWS and an ST2070 reel is necessary. The Alvey sidecaster is also an ideal reel. From a boat the fisherman can either use a Silstar 1100–70SBH rod and an EX2150 reel or a hand line. The line starts at 4-kg breaking strain for the smaller salmon trout to 10 kg for the full adult salmon. In surf use a 90-gram grapple-type sinker or from surf-less beaches a pyramid sinker about 1 metre from the ganged number 1 limerick hooks.

HOW TO CATCH

When using fish flesh, cut fillets about 8 cm long and 1 cm wide. Place the ganged hooks through the top of the bait leaving a tail of about 4 cm.

When using a lure, have only a single number 1 hook. This will catch just as many fish as the jag type, but it is easier to get the hook out on the beach.

Keep the bait moving to attract the salmon. From the boat the speed should be around 2 knots and the line should be about 1 metre under the water. Salmon generally feed at their best on the turn on the high tide,

and feeding seabirds will tell you where they are.

If you are fishing from the shore, try not to use lures as they tend to put the salmon off the bite in a short time. Fresh bait is best. Just for the record, the Australian salmon is not a salmon at all but a perch.

The best places to look for salmon are near rock out-crops which jut out from sandy open beaches and bays. This is where their main food source, whitebait and the like, school and become easy prey for the marauders.

They are a fighting fish with reasonable eating qualities if they are bled as soon as they are caught. I find one of the best methods is to cut the fish's throat and tail, and bury it in the sand for about half an hour. This will drain all of the blood out of the fish.

Another thing is not to catch more than you can use. Salmon are wasted by the thousands each year by over-zealous fishermen. Once you have enough, spool up with ultra-light tackle, say 2 kg, and try your skill. You will lose plenty but it is a great way to teach a new angler how to fish properly.

HOW TO COOK

Salmon is a sought-after fish by anglers, but one which does not have much recognition in the kitchen. However, it is fine when baked with a special stuffing of bread-crumbs, two whole small tomatoes, a whole sliced onion, a clove of garlic, and a shake of basil, paprika, black pepper, parsley flakes, and salt to taste. Place stuffing into the stomach of a salmon of about 2 kg and stitch firmly in with cotton or skewers. Add butter to the outer skin on the back of the fish and wrap it in two layers of foil. Bake at 200°C for about 30 minutes. The stuffing adds flavour and keeps the flesh moist throughout cook-ing. Garnish the salmon with parsley and lemon slices and serve with a French salad.

Samson Fish

LOCATION

Queensland, New South Wales, Victoria, South Australia, and Western Australia.

DESCRIPTION

The samson fish is not unlike the Yellowtail Kingfish. It has a small head and big, powerful body. It is a light grey-green above the lateral line. Its fin and tail structure is not unlike a tuna.

BAIT

Strips of fish flesh or silver lures.

GEAR

Use a top-quality surf rod, such as the Silstar 9912–0BWJ and a heavy duty EX2170 sidecast reel. The rig is a 60-gram bean sinker above a 1-metre trace. Use ganged number 1 limerick hooks.

HOW TO CATCH

The samson fish runs near rocky outcrops in search of food such as pilchards and whitebait. This brings it well into the range of beach and rock fishermen.

For the best results, cast and retrieve all of the time. The retrieval should be fairly fast, as this fish catches prey at high speed.

Set the reel drag carefully, well below the breaking strain. This fish did not get its name for nothing. The initial runs will be fast and furious. Take your time in landing the fish. They are big fish and take a lot of stopping. Gradually increase the drag as the fish tires. Always use a gaff or big landing net. If you know the fish are big in the area, fit a wire trace above the ganged hooks.

HOW TO COOK

Take cutlets of samson fish and place them on a hot barbecue. Turn them quickly and regularly. Mix a paste of butter and finely diced garlic. Baste the cutlets with the paste on either side as you turn the fish. The fish should be basted and turned four times in the five-minute cooking time. Serve with rice topped with parsley.

Sergeant Baker

LOCATION

New South Wales, Victoria, Western Australia. A few have been recently netted offshore in South Australian waters.

DESCRIPTION

The body is not unlike a flathead, but thicker. It has a flat head with a big mouth with spectacular side, belly, and back fins. The tail is strong and fine.

BAIT

Cockles (pipi), prawns, shrimp, worms and whitebait.

GEAR

Try a Silstar 1100–56BWL rod and a heavy duty AT2590 sidecast reel. Use a 10-kg breaking strain line fitted with two number 3/0 beak hooks. A 60-gram pyramid sinker is ideal in most conditions. However, this should be at least 50 cm below the hooks, as the Sergeant Baker is found on reef areas.

HOW TO CATCH

The Sergeant Baker is found mainly on reef areas in about 20 metres of water. However, some have been caught in trawl nets well offshore. They are a good-eating market fish.

Most are caught when the angler is fishing for snapper, so much the same rig as for snapper is ideal. Set the two 3/0 beak hooks on 20-cm traces about 50 cm above a 60-gram pyramid sinker. A sliding rig of a 60-gram bean sinker between the two hooks can also be used. The sinker should be allowed to run about 35 cm.

This fish has a big mouth, therefore the baits should be equally big and sloppy. The mouth is hard and a strong

strike is needed to bed the hook. The Sergeant Baker is only an average fighter, but care should still be taken.

Do not be over anxious in retrieving the fish and use a landing net.

HOW TO COOK

Coat fillets of Sergeant Baker in seasoned flour. This is a big fish, and fillets can be halved or even quartered to fit the pan. Heat butter in a large frying pan and place the fish in the pan. As it is cooking, pour half a cup of red wine over each side. Cook for about 10 minutes or until the flesh starts to flake. Garnish with lemon. Serve with cooked tomato, baby carrots, and boiled new potatoes.

Cocktail
Shark

LOCATION

South Australia, western Victoria, and eastern Western Australia.

DESCRIPTION

Brown to bronze on the back with white eyes, a small head, and thick body. Also known as the Australian Whaler.

BAIT

Whole salmon, big tommy ruff, Rugger Snapper, or small tuna.

GEAR

A light Silstar semi-game rod fitted with a casting reel. The line should be about 12-kg breaking strain with a wire trace and a single 9/0 beak hook.

HOW TO CATCH

The Cocktail Shark is a fish eater which frequents estuaries, bays, and mainly shallow waters in search of schools of fish. Float the baited line out from the boat with a balloon. The trace should be about 3 metres below the balloon. This could be less, depending on the depth of the water. The whaler is a timid shark which will take a good look at a bait before striking.

However, when it does strike, it hits hard and fast. Set the reel drag well under the breaking strain of the line.

When the balloon breaks, strike hard to set the hooks, and be prepared for a long, hard run. These fish have tremendous swimming strength, so at least 300 metres of line should be on the reel. The shark will not fight like a normal scale fish, but will use its weight and bulk to break free. It will make numerous long runs before coming to gaff.

The Cocktail Shark gets its name from the shape of its high cocked tail. Its flesh is clean and white, and is good eating providing the fish is under the 30-kg mark.

HOW TO COOK

Take the cutlets out of the Cocktail Shark and remove the backbone and skin. Soak the cutlets in water with a quarter of a cup of vinegar for half an hour. This will remove any ammonia taste which could have permeated the flesh. Grease a casserole dish with butter and lay in the cutlets. Cover them with slices of tomato and sliced onion, and sprinkle with salt, black pepper, basil, and parsley. Pour on half a cup of tomato paste and cover with thinly sliced potato. Bake in a moderate oven for 45 minutes. Serve with broccoli and carrots.

School
Shark

LOCATION

Southern Australia.

DESCRIPTION

Typical shark body, long and slender with a main fin and a smaller fin near the tail. School Shark come in two species: the Sweet William which has no teeth, and the Snapper Shark which has teeth. They look the same except the Snapper Shark has distinct brown patches on its sides.

BAIT

Fish like tommy ruff, garfish, pilchards, or squid.

GEAR

A semi-game rod like the Silstar 1280 10GAM and a heavy duty AT2570 sidecaster reel. Use a 10-kg breaking strain line. Set a pyramid or star sinker below two 3/0 beak hooks. For added strength, use a light wire trace to the hooks as the Snapper Shark 'schoolies' have small teeth.

HOW TO CATCH

School Shark are caught mainly along limestone reef areas. Their common name in the marketplace is Flake. They feed on small octopus, squid, and fish. Whiting is one of their favourites. Wherever you find a big school of King George Whiting, you will find School Shark.

When fishing for whiting, it always pays to put down a heavy line. I generally bait this with squid head, and this has a twofold benefit. It is a berley for the whiting and a bait for any marauding shark. Be sure that the rod is firmly held in a holder on the boat, because when a shark takes the bait it will run fiercely.

Generally, however, you will know when a shark is at the bait. They pick at the bait in the same way as a snapper and the line will bounce. Be sure that the drag on the reel is set well below the breaking strain of the line.

Clear all other lines out of the water as soon as you know the shark is at the bait. It only takes one run for the shark to have the lot. Always let the shark tire right out. This could mean you bring it to the boat several times and down it will go again. It will lie still when the fight is out of it.

Use a gaff and have a mallet handy. Use one gaff action over the fish near the head. Once aboard, strike the shark with the mallet on the nose. Sharks have no bones, only gristle, and this will shatter the back structure and kill the shark. On the way in take the head off and the gut out. Shark have ammonia in their body and as the fish dies this is expelled into the flesh. The backbone structure should also come out.

HOW TO COOK

Flake is the no-bone fish of the sea. First the fillets of flake should be soaked in a solution of two parts vinegar to eight parts water for an hour. Cover the fillets completely. This will remove any ammonia taste in the flesh. Boil the flesh with the spider of a crayfish until it goes flakey but firm. Dice the fish into small flakes and put in a baking dish. Sprinkle breadcrumbs, shallots, mixed herbs, and butter on the top and place it in an oven at about 200°C. This should take about 30 minutes.

Snapper

LOCATION

Australia wide.

DESCRIPTION

Deep red above the lateral line and a white belly. Big, blunt head with large eyes and big back spines.

BAIT

Fresh prawns, crabs, squid, and small fish such as pilchards, tommy ruffs, salmon trout, or bluebait.

GEAR

The breaking strain of line varies from 5-kg for sports fishing to 30-kg breaking strain for hand lining. However, the lighter the line the better depending on the size of the fish in the school. For a rod try the all new Silstar 1280 66WB fitted with an AX2650 reel. This will give perfect balance and control no matter how big the snapper. Use a rig similar to whiting, only heavier. A 90-gram sliding bean sinker between two number 3/0 beak hooks. Again the hook size and sinker size can vary with the size of the fish and fishing conditions. Fish as light as possible.

HOW TO CATCH

The main haunt of snapper is deep, offshore reef areas where their natural food source is plentiful. However, the adult fish migrate regularly into shallow waters to spawn. This is the time they start feeding on crabs, prawns, and the like, and come within easy reach of the average angler. They feed mainly at night and generally go in big schools. They are constantly hunted by small sharks and this makes them always touchy and hard to hold near a boat in shallow waters. Therefore, it is essential that no noise comes from the boat and there are no lights shining on the water. Never clean and gut snapper in shallow

waters where you fish. The smell of their blood in the water alerts them to a shark in the area and the school will split up and vanish.

The baits should be big and sloppy, and in the case of big snapper, over 10 kg, stale and smelly. Smaller snapper prefer fresh bait. When a snapper first takes a bait, you will feel slight picks. Let the snapper have a little loose line, about 1 metre, so that it can get the bait well down and run.

When the run starts, strike hard so that the hook is well set. Snapper have a very hard mouth. Do not be too anxious in getting the fish to gaff. Take your time; they are big fish with tremendous power. At times during the fight you will feel that the fish is finished. This is only a ploy to get rid of the hook. It will swim easy up towards you, then all of a sudden fight back with short sharp jerks. This is when it is important to keep the tip of the rod well up so that it can take the shock without harm to the line. When the fish has lost all fight it will lay on its side. This is the time to bring out the gaff or landing net. When gaffing the snapper always go over the fish, never underneath, and with a landing net take the fish head first, never from the tail.

When gilling and gutting snapper always check their stomachs to find out what they are naturally feeding on. This should be your bait next time out.

HOW TO COOK

Select a whole snapper about 2 kg. Carefully clean any blood from around the exposed backbone as this can give the flesh a bitter taste. Stuff the stomach with seeded grapes, green or red, and stitch tightly with cotton or skewers. Wrap the fish in two layers of foil after adding a liberal lacing of butter to the upper skin. Place it in the oven at 200°C for about 30 minutes.

Snook

LOCATION

Southern Australia.

DESCRIPTION

A long, slender fish with a large mouth and rows of small, sharp teeth. Light copper on the back, silver on the sides, and a white underbelly. Also known as pike.

BAIT

Fillets of fish such as garfish, mackerel, tommy ruff, or the Halco snook lure.

GEAR

This is essentially a troll fish, but rods can be used when a big school is located. Use a Silstar 1100–90BWS and an EX2160 reel fitted with a 8-kg breaking strain line and a Halco snook lure for spinning for snook. A paravane can be used when trolling, but this is only successful with lures. I prefer the old and tested leaded snook line. This is made from a 40-kg main line fitted with 12-gram barrel sinker leads, spaced about 25 cm apart. There should be 7 kg of barrel sinkers on the line. Attach a 7-metre trace of 10-kg breaking strain line to the main line. If you are using the snook lure, remove the grapple type hooks and replace them with a single number 2 limerick hook. This will allow the lure to work better and the fish are easier to get off.

If bait is used, ganged number 2 hooks are required. The baits should be about 8-cm long, 1-cm wide, and very thin. Use a sharp knife, and place the two hooks in the fillet so that the grain of the flesh runs to the tail of the bait. This tail should hang about 4 cm from the bottom hook. When you are fastening the leads, do not pinch them from the ends. This will cut the line. Give them a sharp tap with a hammer to secure them safely.

HOW TO CATCH

Snook bite best at first light and just before dusk. A school can generally be located by watching the feeding seabirds. Once the school is located, it is important to find the centre. By using two troll lines this is easy, as snook will be hooked at the same time on both lines. As soon as this happens, drop a marker. From then on simply troll around the marker or anchor nearby and start spinning with the rods.

When using bait, the boat speed should be about 1 knot and the line is worked back and forth with a 'jag-and-let-go action'. If a fish strikes and is not hooked, drop the line back quickly. The snook has tasted the fish and thinks it has killed it if the bait stops quickly in the water. The snook will then come up and take it.

When using a lure, the boat speed is about 2 knots and the line is held still so that the lure can really work in the water. When the fish strikes, do not jag or you will pull the lure out of its mouth. Wait until you feel the weight of the fish and then pull in.

Snook enter Port Phillip Bay in summer and move right along southern Australia year round. In winter they are in deeper water and in summer the gulf and estuaries.

Some may query the breaking strain of the lines, but these have a twofold job. The same lines are also used for locating schools of snapper when the big reds are hard to find. The only thing that changes is the size of hooks and baits—both are bigger.

HOW TO COOK

Chop pieces of snook into 3 cm cubes. Roll the cubes in a self-raising flour, egg and milk batter. Deep fry in hot cooking oil for about three minutes. Serve with salad.

Squid

LOCATION

Worldwide. Their size ranges from a few grams to the Giant Squid of several hundred kilograms which sperm whales feed on.

DESCRIPTION

There are two species. The Torpedo Squid has a slender body with two short side flaps on either side of the rear end of the squid. It has a smaller head and tentacles than the Native Squid. The Native Squid has flaps the full length of the body, big eyes, and long tentacles. The two main tentacles are roughly four times longer than the remaining holding tentacles. Both species have sharp parrot-like beaks in the centre of the tentacles. They can change colour to suit the environment.

BAIT

Whole small fish like garfish, tommy ruffs, or mullet, or modern lures. These lures come in different sizes and look and act like a shrimp in the water.

GEAR

Most squid are caught on a handline. Use about a 10-kg breaking strain line and fit the jig, jag, or lure without any sinker.

HOW TO CATCH

Squid for years was considered only a bait for other fish. However, this has all changed with the influx of European and Asian migrants to Australia.

It is one of the cleanest and easiest fish in the sea to catch. I prefer the jig to a jag. The difference in these two rigs is that a jag has barbs on the hooks and a jig is a series of barbless points. The jig is a 'never miss' rig if handled properly. When the squid takes the bait, it naturally pulls

back and hooks itself on the spikes. All the angler has to do is keep weight on the squid and it cannot get free. In the case of a jag, there are less hooks and these have to be sunk into a tentacle.

The lures operate the same way as the jig. A squid takes them, hooks himself, and all the angler has to do is pull it in without giving any slack line.

During spawning time, generally from October to December in southern waters, the squid feed in and around inshore reef areas. These are not the big rocky reefs but patches of limestone and coral near shore.

There are two basic methods of catching squid. One, the lazy man's way, is to leave a baited squid jig about 1 metre from the sea floor while you fish for other fish. Tie the line to a bucket handle and when the bucket moves you know you have a squid.

The other is to cast the lure about 20 metres from the boat, let it sink for a few seconds, and then slowly retrieve. Squid will follow and take the bait. Always use a landing net and leave the squid over the side until it has squirted all of its ink. Many a summer fashion has been ruined by squid ink.

HOW TO COOK

Squid (calamari) is one of the cleanest and easiest fish to cook. Slice the squid into thin strips or rings. Heat butter in the frying pan until it is very hot. Put the strips in and stir them to be sure they are covered with butter. Add a dash of salt, pepper, basil, and paprika and stir again. Turn the heat down to medium. Add soya sauce and put a lid over the pan. The total cooking time is no more than three minutes. The squid must not pop in the pan. If it does it is going hard and will be tough to eat. Serve as an entree or a main course with mashed potato or rice, carrots, beans, and broccoli.

Sweep

LOCATION

South Australia, southern Victoria, Tasmania, and Western Australia.

DESCRIPTION

Steely grey with dark bands. A thin upright fish with a small head, deep body, and fine fin structure.

BAIT

Cockles (pipi), crushed squid, worms, shrimp, and fish flesh.

GEAR

Use a Silstar 1100–120BWH surf rod from the rocks with an AT2590 reel or a 1100–66SP rod and an EX2150 reel from a boat. From rocks, a small bob or quill float should be set about a metre above a single number 4 beak hook. From a boat, use a free floating line with a similar hook. If the tide is running add a small lead shot, just to get the bait down. If you are fishing from rocks where there is an ocean swell be careful—do not go on wet rocks.

HOW TO CATCH

There is nothing a sweep likes more than rough, turbulent water among rocks. This is where its food source lies, as well as protection from predators.

Allow the baits to drift in the most turbulent part of the waters. Leave plenty of loose line so that the sweep can 'play' with the bait, then as the slack tightens, strike. The sweep has a small mouth but it is firm and hard, so a firm strike is necessary. Use about 5-kg breaking strain line for the best results.

Sweep will give a good fight, so it is wise to set the drag on the reel well below the breaking strain. They will

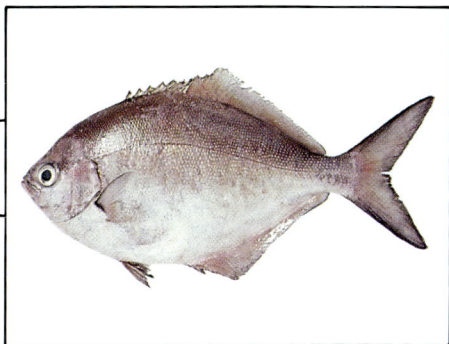

circle as they are coming up, so try to gauge your lift as the fish is going away from you.

Other areas where sweep will be found are lagoons inside surf-tossed reefs. One such reef is Dangerous Reef in South Australia's Spencer Gulf, and another is at the northern end of Wardang Island. However, the biggest sweep come from areas like Port Fairy and Portland in Victoria, King and Flinders islands off Tasmania, and the West Coast of South Australia.

They make fine eating, but are not seen in the market place often because they are difficult to catch in commercial quantities.

HOW TO COOK

Fish like the sweep can be tasty when cooked whole. In most cases they are best cooked in butter. This brings out the natural flavour of the fish. Roll the fish, minus the head, in flour so that it will not stick to the pan. Use a hot pan. The fish should be cooked for about four minutes on either side. At the last minute pour some white wine over the fish, turn the heat off, and let them simmer for another minute to get the wine flavour through the flesh. Serve with chips, beans, and carrots and garnish with parsley and lemon.

Sweetlip

LOCATION

Northern New South Wales, especially the Great Barrier Reef.

DESCRIPTION

Pink tipped fins, grey-purple body, small head with a protruding mouth and a strong, thick tail. Also known as Emperor.

BAIT

Shrimp, squid, cockles (pipi), and octopus pieces.

GEAR

Try a Silstar 1100 66BWJ rod with a ST2070 reel. The line should be about 8-kg breaking strain with two 2/0 hooks above a 60-gram pyramid sinker.

HOW TO CATCH

The sweetlip is a game fighter and must be treated with respect. Most caught on the Barrier Reef weigh in around 3 kg, but they can be as big as 12 kg.

They have a strong mouth. When the bite is felt strike hard to penetrate the firm flesh.

Unlike many fish on the reef, they bite quite freely and take a wide variety of baits.

Fish in the deeper holes of the reef. Once hooked get the fish off the bottom as quickly as possible as it has a habit of diving for the nearest cover. Always have a second spool of heavier breaking strain line in case a school of bigger sweetlip are located. About 12 kg would be ideal. Keep the rod up once the fish is hooked and let the tip of the rod do the work. Always use a landing net to bag the fish.

The sweetlip has a fine eating flesh but it should always be stored in a cool place on the boat.

HOW TO COOK

Take a whole sweetlip and place in an oven-proof dish. Surround the fish with small tomatoes and champignons. Add half a cup of cooking oil and a few dobs of butter. Sprinkle the fish with black pepper and salt. Bake for about 25 minutes in a 200°C oven. Sprinkle with parsley just before taking the fish from the oven. Serve with the salad in season.

Tailor

LOCATION

New South Wales, Victoria, Tasmania, South Australia, Western Australia, and Queensland.

DESCRIPTION

Not unlike a salmon. A yellow-silver colour, strong tail, and the back fins are set well back from the head. It has sharp teeth which leave an incision like a pair of tailor's scissors, hence the name. In some areas they are known as choppers.

BAIT

Strips of fish flesh like garfish, salmon trout, or small mackerel or whitebait, pilchards and anchovy. Silver lures can also be used.

GEAR

A surf rod similar to the Silstar 1200–120BWL and an AX2670 sidecast reel. Use about 8-kg breaking strain line. I find a trolling rig is best, with a 60-gram bean sinker set above a 1-metre trace. A wire leader should be added to the trace. Ganged number 2 limerick hooks would be ideal.

HOW TO CATCH

Tailor move down the eastern seaboard in great numbers. They average around the 2-kg mark but bigger fish are caught. They run in schools similar to salmon and, when they are on the bite, they will snap at anything that moves. However, the biggest tailor are caught on the West Coast of South Australia. Here 4-kg tailor are common and many are bigger but the schools are not as big as on the eastern seaboard. Most of the big fish are caught with schools of salmon.

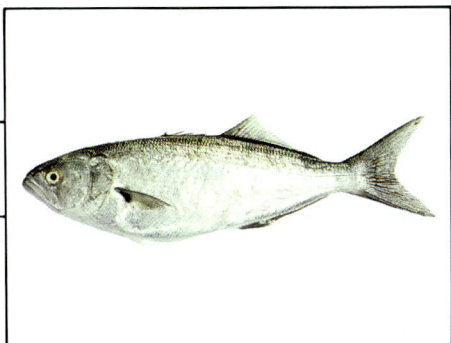

When fishing for tailor from the rocks, take care. Do not venture on to wet rocks. Cast well out into the school and retrieve. The retrieval should be fairly fast. Set the drag well below the breaking strain of the line. Tailor are one of the gamest fighters in the sea, so take your time bringing the fish in.

Bleed the fish by cutting the throat and around the tail as soon as possible.

For the beginner, try the backwaters first before venturing on to the rocks. Here you will gain experience which will make your tailor fishing safer and more enjoyable.

HOW TO COOK

Take fillets of tailor. Roll the fillets in flour, then dip in beaten egg, and finally roll in crushed cornflakes until each is liberally covered. Heat cooking oil in the pan. The oil should be very hot. Slice bananas full length. Put the fish and the bananas in the pan and cook for about three or four minutes. Serve the fish and banana side by side, and garnish with slices of lemon and parsley.

Tarwhine

LOCATION

Queensland, New South Wales, and parts of Western Australia.

DESCRIPTION

Not unlike a bream to look at, though the head is more rounded and the back fin begins further down the back. It is silver with traces of yellow in colour, and has a broad tail.

BAIT

Worms, whitebait, cockles (pipi), and small pieces of squid.

GEAR

A light, fine tipped rod about 2 metres in length like the Silstar 1280 66SP and an AT2540 reel is ideal. The rig should be the same as for bream: a light 30-gram sliding sinker above a 1-metre trace with one or two number 3 beak hooks.

HOW TO CATCH

The tarwhine is a wary fish and all care should be taken with baits and gear. The sinker must be able to slide freely so that the fish does not feel any weight and the hooks should be covered with bait, taking care not to snag the point of the hook on a hard piece of flesh. The bait should be big and, when using worms, a tail should be left hanging. The line should be no more than 4-kg breaking strain for beginners and lighter for the experts.

Leave plenty of loose line so that the fish can run before striking the hook. Strike hard, as the tarwhine has a hard mouth.

The tarwhine is found in estuaries, rivers, and bays along the coast. The best time to fish is at dawn and dusk.

HOW TO COOK

Take a whole tarwhine and clean thoroughly. Prepare a stuffing of breadcrumbs, melted butter, chopped parsley, finely chopped celery leaves, and the juice of garlic. Put the stuffing into the stomach of the fish and stitch. Put the fish in a pre-heated oven of about 200°C. A 2-kg fish will take about 25 minutes to cook. Serve with fresh tomato, slices of onion, and mashed potato.

Teraglin

LOCATION

Northern New South Wales, Queensland, and northern Western Australia.

DESCRIPTION

The teraglin has a broad, flat tail, small head, and a large mouth. It has a thick body with a double row of fins on the back.

BAIT

Whitebait, fish pieces, prawns, shrimp, and crushed squid.

GEAR

Try a Silstar 1280 66SP or similar rod and an AT2550 sidecast reel. The line should be about 10-kg breaking strain. Use two 2/0 hooks above and below a 60-gram sliding bean sinker. The sinker should be allowed to slide about 30 cm.

HOW TO CATCH

This fish is found mainly in deep water, 20 metres upwards, but it does occasionally come into shallow estuaries in search of prawns. In the estuary areas the best times to fish are at night.

Select baits which will completely fill the hook, keeping in mind that the point of the hook must not be snagged. This will give each bait a more natural look.

This fish prefers a sandy or mud bottom, therefore the angler can slowly lift and drop the bait so that it looks alive. Once the fish is hooked, keep the rod at about 45 degrees to the water so that the tip can take any extra strain the fish may apply in its early runs. See that the drag on the reel is set under the line's breaking strain and gradually apply pressure as the fish tires. Keep the weight

on the fish all of the time. A loose line for a second is enough to lose the fish.

Use a landing net when boating the fish.

HOW TO COOK

Fillets of teraglin are ideal when poached or boiled. Boil water and add salt to taste. As the water boils, place the fillets in and leave to simmer (not boil) for about 10 minutes, or until cooked if the fillets are very thick. Serve with parsley sauce, steamed cabbage, and sliced onions and carrots.

Threadfin

LOCATION

Northern Territory, Queensland, and northern Western Australia.

DESCRIPTION

The threadfin has a body similar to the Southern Salmon, though the tail is larger and finer. The head is similar to a Rainbow Trout or Sockeye Salmon. They are not related to the southern species. The threadfin grows to 120 kg. Many in Australia have touched the 50-kg mark. Also known as Northern Salmon.

BAIT

Small, live fish like mullet, and fish fillets.

GEAR

Use a Silstar semi-game rod fitted with a top quality casting reel. The line should be at least 10-kg breaking strain fitted with ganged 4/0 limerick hooks. A single 4/0 beak hook is used with live bait.

HOW TO CATCH

The threadfin is found in estuaries and rivers in northern Australia. It can be trolled for in the same way as the Southern Salmon, with fish fillets on two ganged hooks.

However, live bait is a natural for these fighting fish. A single number 4/0 beak hook is placed through the back of a mullet, taking care not to harm the lateral line, and the fish allowed to swim freely on a loose line. Mulloway are caught in the same way.

These fish feed in the same way as the Southern Salmon, so feeding sea birds will tell where the schools are. They are, however, better fighters than their southern counterparts. Once hooked, all hell breaks loose for the angler. Drags scream and the line runs at tremendous speed, so

be sure that the drag has been carefully preset. Keep the rod up all the time, so that the tip can do its proper job.

In my opinion, this fish puts up a far greater fight than the barramundi, and its eating qualities are almost as good.

HOW TO COOK

Place big fillets of threadfin in a well-buttered, ovenproof dish. Add slices of shallots or finely sliced onion, basil, parsley flakes, and whole small or sliced tomatoes, champignons, diced celery, and half a cup of lemon juice. Bake in a moderate oven for about 20 minutes. Just before the dish is ready, sprinkle the fish with grated cheese and allow the cheese to melt. Serve with creamed potato, small zucchini, and diced carrots.

Tommy Ruff

LOCATION

Southern Australia.

DESCRIPTION

Steely grey in colour, with a big dark eye and black tips to the tail. Similar in shape to salmon trout.

BAIT

Gents (maggots), whitebait, mince berley, crayfish tail, fish flesh.

GEAR

A fine-tipped 3-metre rod similar to the Silstar 1100–100BWS with an EX2150 reel for fishing from a pier or jetty, and a Silstar 1280 66SP with an EX2150 sidecast reel from a boat is ideal. From a boat, two number 9 limerick hooks floating free, with no floats, is ideal. From a jetty, use a 30-gram spring sinker below three number 9 limerick hooks.

HOW TO CATCH

The tommy ruff is a real fun fish for the amateur. For their size, they are game little fighters and when in a feeding frenzy can be caught by the dozen. At night they come close inshore in search of food, and this is when the shore angler comes into his own. In South Australia places like Edithburgh, Penneshaw, and Port Giles throng with hundreds of eager anglers as soon as the sun goes down.

When fishing from a pier or jetty, it is important to remember that the tommy ruff likes a moving bait. Therefore the line should be lifted and dropped at regular intervals. The fish will generally bite on the uplift.

When the fish strikes, there is no need to jag—just keep lifting the line and reel in. Tommy ruffs have a very

brittle mouth and by jagging it is more often than not broken and the fish lost. Some anglers prefer the smaller number 11 hooks for tommy ruff. I prefer the bigger hooks, as the fish is less likely to swallow them completely.

Berley should be used, but it must be kept to a trickle. It should be made into a paste which clings tightly to the springs in the sinker. I find that beef mince laced with a can of sardines and bread is the best. Always try to fish as near to the jetty as possible. You should never have to cast out more than a few metres.

From a boat, tommy ruff are caught in the same manner as garfish. Two number 9 hooks on a free line is enough. More often than not the tommies will arrive in the boat's berley stream before the garfish. Do not try to hook them by jagging. Let them hook themselves.

Like mullet, their flesh will deteriorate very quickly if they are not kept cool. To clean them, simply cut through the backbone behind the gills and tear the head from the body. All of the gut will come out with the head.

The best time to fish is during the summer months when there are more slightly smaller fish about. The really big ones come in during winter, but not in such great numbers. If you intend using gents for bait, be sure that they have been bred from fish scraps, this gives the bait a more natural taste to the fish. Hook the gents to the hook from the 'blunt end' of the gent, so that the thinner head can wriggle on the hook.

HOW TO COOK

Take tommy ruff fillets and wrap in thin bacon slices. Wrap the fish in foil and place under the griller for about 10 minutes. A dob of butter can be added to the fish before cooking, but there is generally ample oil in the bacon. Serve with a French salad.

Trevally

LOCATION

Queensland, New South Wales, Victoria, Tasmania, and South Australia.

DESCRIPTION

There are several species. The most common has a blue-silver back turning to a yellow-green on the sides near the lateral line, and a small head. A very deep, streamlined fish.

BAIT

Fish flesh, cockles (pipi), crushed squid, pilchards, whitebait, and shrimp.

GEAR

From the shore use a surf rod similar to the Silstar 999–120BWS and an EX2170 reel. From a boat the 1100–56 BWM is ideal with an AT 2540 reel. The line should be about 8-kg breaking strain for big fish down to about 4 kg for smaller. Use a conventional pyramid sinker below two number 4 beak hooks for the smaller trevally and raise the hook size to 3/0 for bigger fish.

HOW TO CATCH

Trevally are found on reef areas and wrecks around the coastline. Surging water around rocks does not bother them, in fact it helps them in their hunt for food.

Keep the sinker about 50 cm from the hooks to avoid snagging on the rocks. If the reef is exposed, try using a bob float with the hooks about 2 metres below.

Always use big bait and, in this case, leave the points of the hooks exposed. Trevally like to suck a bait into their mouths, therefore the bite is generally lighter than you would expect from a big fish. They have a very weak

mouth structure so it is important to get the hook well down the throat, especially when the fish are big.

When a trevally is hooked, be prepared for a fight. They are a strong fish. Their habit when hooked is to lie on their side and swim in big circles. This exposes the greater part of their body to the water pressure and makes them difficult to lift. It also puts strain on the side of their mouth which is very brittle.

No matter what size the trevally is, use a landing net or gaff when landing the fish. The trevally is a fine eating fish, but the flesh will go soft if left exposed to sunshine too long. Keep them covered with a wet bag.

HOW TO COOK

Take a butterfly fillet of trevally and paint both sides with butter and lemon. Finely dice parsley, carrot, cheese, onion, and add fresh ground black pepper. Mix the ingredients thoroughly. Place this on one side of the fillet and fold the other over the top. Skewer in two or three places with tooth picks and place in a well-oiled baking dish. Cook for about 25 minutes in a hot oven, about 190°C. Serve with boiled small potatoes, carrots, and beans.

Brown
Trout

LOCATION

New South Wales, Victoria, Tasmania, South Australia, and southern Western Australia.

DESCRIPTION

The Brown Trout's head is small in comparison with its deep brown body. It has a typical trout beak-type mouth.

BAIT

Yabbies, worms, freshwater shrimp, small fish, and for the purist a range of trout flies.

GEAR

For a rod try the new Silstar 1200−90FL fitted with an JWY1530 reel. Shorter, flexible rods can be used, especially when trolling for trout in places like Lake Gordon and Lake Pedder in southern Tasmania.

HOW TO CATCH

The Brown Trout grows to a big size, so big that in Tasmania they claim they have the biggest in the world in their south-western lakes system. I personally have boated and released a 8-kg monster in Lake Pedder. On the same day we caught one which weighed in at more than 10-kg. They were caught on a spoon-type lure. No live bait is allowed in Lake Gordon or Lake Pedder. For lures try the Abu Killer or even a silver wobbler with a touch of red and green on it. Like their close cousin the Rainbow Trout, the Brown likes deep holes near rocks with water flowing over them or just downstream from river rapids.

However, they are just as at home in the quieter waters of lakes. This is where the really big ones are. Here they like a moving bait, so keep casting and slowly retrieving.

In New South Wales and Victorian rivers stemming from the Alps, Brown Trout are prolific in spring and autumn. South Australia has only a few streams but Tasmania is blessed with some of the best trout fishing in the world. The upper reaches of the Derwent River, the Shannon and Ouse rivers, the Great Lakes and, of course, the southern lakes, are all loaded with the great fighting fish.

For the beginner, try using an 8-kg breaking strain line and, as your knowledge grows, go lighter and on to the special tapered trout lines. The best time to fish is just before a change in the weather, when the insects are buzzing about the waters.

HOW TO COOK

Soft-flesh fish like Brown Trout can be successfully fried if the flesh is cooked quickly. Roll the fillets in a batter of flour, milk, and egg. Mix the batter so that it is stiff; this will help to tighten the flesh. Have the oil at boiling point when the fillets are inserted. A deep fry is best. Cook until the batter becomes a golden brown. This should take about three minutes. Top the fish with finely grated cheese, parsley, and lemon slices. Serve with salads of the day.

Coral
Trout

LOCATION

Queensland, Northern Territory, and northern Western Australia.

DESCRIPTION

Short, thick head with a large mouth. Eyes set close in the top of the head. Broad, strong tail. Pink on the underbelly to purple on the back. However, colours can vary.

BAIT

Whitebait, pilchards, bluebait, strips of fish flesh.

GEAR

A semi-game rod like the Silstar 1280 10JIG and a top quality AX2650 reel is needed to land these powerful fish. Use a 15-kg breaking strain line. The trace should have a 60-gram pyramid sinker below two 4/0 beak hooks.

HOW TO CATCH

Coral Trout have weighed in at more than 20 kg. This makes them a very powerful fish. When fishing for Coral Trout keep the bait moving. This can be done by either drifting slowly over the coral or lifting and dropping the line while at anchor.

Cut up some small fish and berley the area before fishing. This will attract the trout under the boat. Set the reel drag well under the line-breaking strain. Hold the rod or put it in a firm rod holder. Many a rod has gone over the side with a hooked Coral Trout.

Like catching all big fish, take your time once the hook is bedded in. A fish tires quicker when it is allowed to run well away from the boat. It means the fish not only has to fight you at the end of the rod, but it also has to drag line through the water. This dragging line tires a fish quicker than anything else.

Use a landing net or gaff. If you are using a net, take the fish head first.

HOW TO COOK

Here is a recipe for the camper. Take a big Coral Trout or similar fish and clean and gut it. Dig a hole in the ground, about a metre square, and light a strong fire in the bottom of it. Keep adding to the fire until there is a thick layer of coals exposed. Add some butter, salt, and pepper to the fish. Wrap the fish in two layers of foil and about 10 layers of wet newspaper. Put a thin layer of sand over the coals and place the fish on top. Cover the fish in sand and go fishing for a few hours (up to four). Dig up the fish and it is cooked and ready for a great meal.

Rainbow
Trout

LOCATION

New South Wales, Victoria, South Australia, Tasmania, and Western Australia.

DESCRIPTION

A fish with a strong body and small head with a distinct beak on the lip. Side colours range from light pink to brown and purple with some blue patches.

BAIT

For the amateurs it is tiger worms, freshwater shrimp, and yabbies, but for the purist it is a wide variety of artificial flies.

GEAR

This is one fish where the correct gear goes a long way in getting fish. First you must have a proper trout rod, like the Silstar 1200–90FL and a JWY1530 reel. This will give the maximum flexibility and whip for casting. Start off with a 4-kg breaking strain line and a single un-weighted, thin gauge number 5 limerick hook. Later you will graduate to the tapered line for easy casting.

HOW TO CATCH

Rainbow Trout like running water and in most cases make their territory in deep pools below rocks in the stream where the water is constantly aerated. During the day they stay close to the banks as they watch for food going past. Here they are easily frightened. A heavy footstep or bright coloured clothing is enough to send them scurrying away. Quietness is essential, as even the rustle of reeds can affect the fish. The best time to fish is just before a cool change when the insects start skimming the water. Moths, flies, and other flying creatures are all in the diet of the trout.

Cast well into the stream and let the bait sink slowly. If the stream is flowing fast, try casting where the water falls over the rocks and let the bait flow down with the gurgling current. This makes the bait look a lot more natural to the fish. The trout will strike quickly, so be well prepared for it with a loose drag on the reel. Keep the rod up and keep strain on the fish all of the time.

Use a landing net—do not try to lift the fish on to the bank. And do not be discouraged if you do not have success at the first outing. They are a hard fish to catch at any time, even by the experts.

HOW TO COOK

Take a whole Rainbow Trout and fill the gut cavity with onion slices, a few black peppers, and three sprigs of fresh thyme. Wrap the fish in foil and place on a hot barbecue. Open the foil and test the fish after five minutes and at regular intervals thereafter. When it is nearly cooked, paint the fish with butter, and reseal. Cook a further two minutes.

Trumpeter

LOCATION

All states of Australia.

DESCRIPTION

Small head, large body, and small tail. Silver body with brown, full-length stripes.

BAIT

Cockles (pipi), squid, worms, or shrimp.

GEAR

A light rod like the Silstar 999–60SP and an ST2040 reel to match. Use a 4-kg breaking strain line with a conventional rig of pyramid sinker below two or three number 8 limerick hooks.

HOW TO CATCH

The trumpeter is found in shallow estuaries and bays during the summer months. At most times they are a nuisance when other fish are about. They get to the baits first almost every time. However, they are great sport for youngsters learning to fish. Their bite is sharp, and this teaches a youngster to react quickly. In summer months they will bite all day and night. They also make ideal bait for snapper, mulloway, and crabs.

I find the best hooking method is similar to tommy ruff fishing. Keep lifting the line until the fish strikes, then reel in. Adults should take the fish off the hooks for the youngsters to start with, as they are very spiny. Show them how to hold the fish flat.

Trumpeter were once considered a rubbish fish, but in recent years they have found their way into the marketplace.

HOW TO COOK

If you like vinegar in your fish, and cannot stand the bones, try covering the rough fillets in vinegar in a dish overnight. The vinegar will dissolve the bones and turn the flesh white. Drain off the vinegar and allow the fillets to dry. Roll them in a stiff batter and deep fry. This is ideal for trumpeter.

Tuna

LOCATION

All Australian states though the species differs slightly from the Southern Bluefin to the Stripy Tuna, Northern Bluefin, Yellowfin, and others.

DESCRIPTION

One of the most streamlined fish in the sea, built for speed and strength. It has a small head, big eyes, and a slender tail structure. Even the fins fit into grooves in the body for less water resistance.

BAIT

Pilchards, anchovy, and garfish, though most are caught on lures by amateur fishermen. These range from a simple feather lure with a 4/0 beak hook to imitation squid and heavy 100-gram silky wobbler-type lures. I find the imitation squid as good as any, especially when the inside of the squid is packed with cotton wool and soaked in fish oil.

GEAR

Try the Silstar 1280 10JIG rod fitted with an AX2660 sidecast reel. This rod gives the whip and strength to hold the biggest fish and the reel is geared just right for the big fish. The line should be no less than 10-kg breaking strain for the beginner.

HOW TO CATCH

Tuna swim in schools, feeding as they go, and much of this time is near the surface. These schools can be located by the seabirds feeding on the leftovers from the small fish the tuna are eating. The fish will jump clear of the water when in a feeding frenzy.

The main thing to remember when trolling for tuna is that each school has a lead fish which, if disturbed, will

sound, go to deep water, and the whole school will follow. Therefore, it is important to first ascertain which way the school is travelling and be sure not to cut across its path. Do so and you have lost the school.

Once you know their direction, move into the side of the school at about 9 knots and have the lines set on top of the water, on the back of the second stern wave about 20 metres astern. The tuna will be attracted to the wash of the boat. Be sure the reel's drag is set well below the line's breaking strain, as once the fish is hooked it will run and fight harder than any fish in the sea.

In the first stages of the fight, just try to contain the fish. As the line goes further out it will tire. Keep the rod well up so that it can take all of the shock of the fast, fighting runs. Take your time; you have a real fish on the end of the line and it will not give up without a terrific struggle. Play the fish right out until it starts to lie on its side, before using the gaff or landing net. Sink the gaff over the top of the fish as near to the head as possible. If you are using a big landing net, take the fish head first, not from the tail.

When you clean and gut the tuna, do not sink the knife right to the backbone. They are one of the few fish in the sea with meat right around the backbone.

HOW TO COOK

One of the best fish for the barbecue is the tuna. Get the plate very hot. Pour beer on the plate and let it steam just before putting 2 cm thick tuna cutlets on it. Drop the cutlets on the plate and pour more beer over it. Seal the underside and turn (about 10 seconds), then pour on more beer. Each pour should be about half a cup. It will take about five minutes each side.

Turrum

LOCATION

Queensland and the Northern Territory.

DESCRIPTION

Not unlike a trevally in shape and skin texture. It has a blue-grey back with fine yellow-brown stripes, a fine tail, and small head.

BAIT

Strips of fish like garfish or pike or big silver lures.

GEAR

This fish is caught by trolling in most cases. Use a semi-game rod like the Silstar 1280 66BWB and an AX2670 sidecast reel. The line should be about 12-kg breaking strain with a wire trace. The hooks can range from 3/0 to 5/0 beak and a 60-gram bean sinker is placed at the tip of the trace to give the line some depth when trolling.

HOW TO CATCH

The boat speed should be about 2 knots for the turrum. When using a silver lure, do not work the line. Let the lure do this work for you.

When bait is used, a forward and back action on the line will make the bait look more realistic to the fish. The bait strips should be about 10 cm long and 2 cm wide and cut thinly. Leave a good length tail hanging behind the hooks. This will flap in the water and attract the fish.

The turrum is a real fighting fish, so care should be taken. They weigh in at about 15 kg at times. By the way, do not be surprised if a Spanish Mackerel takes the bait. They hunt in the same waters.

HOW TO COOK

Baked turrum laced with garlic makes a delightful meal. Slice pockets in the back of the fish and place a clove of garlic in each pocket. Liquify some butter and pour over and into each pocket. Wrap the fish in two layers of foil. Heat the oven to 200°C before placing the fish in the oven. Cook for about 30 minutes, depending on the size of the fish. Garnish with parsley and slices of lemon. Serve with mashed potatoes, carrots and beans.

King George
Whiting

LOCATION

South Australia, southern Victoria, southern Western Australia.

DESCRIPTION

Light brown to grey, with dark brown spots above the lateral line. A bottom feeder with a distinct migration pattern. Also known as Spotted Whiting.

BAIT

Cockles (pipi), squid, sea worms, cuttlefish, and shrimp.

GEAR

A Silstar 1280 60SP rod fitted with an AX2640 sidecast reel is ideal for boat and estuary fishing. The 1·8-metre rod has plenty of action at the tip to hook the fish easily, and the remainder of the rod is stiff enough to give the angler control over the fish.

Use about 6-kg breaking strain line for all-purpose fishing. The best rig is a 30-gram bean sinker between two number 5 hooks. The sinker should be allowed to slide about 40 cm. By using this rig you allow the whiting to feel the bait without any sinker or line weight. A 30-gram pyramid sinker below two number 5 hooks is also used at times, especially in deep water, that is, over 12 metres. Use only limerick hooks.

HOW TO CATCH

King George Whiting start their life in shallow estuary waters such as Spencer and St Vincent gulfs in South Australia, and Port Phillip Bay in Victoria. In their early stages they feed mainly on worms and small shellfish. They will stay in these waters for about two years. As they reach maturity, over 30 cm, they migrate into deeper, colder waters. Their habitat and feed patterns change to small squid, shrimp, and green weed berries such as cork weed. These are found on limestone reef areas off-shore.

Such reefs are rarely in waters over 20 metres deep.

Cover the hook completely with bait, but be sure that the point of the hook is not snagged on a hard piece of flesh. When baiting with cockles, place the black body of the cockle near the point of the hook. This is what the whiting will go for first. When fishing with squid, beat the flesh to a pulp and dip in squid ink to give it a natural smell to the whiting. The reason for this is that the young squid on which the whiting feed are almost a jelly and your bait must be the same.

Generally, the annual migration of the adult fish starts in April and continues through winter. The best time to fish is half an hour before and after the change of tide, when small sea creatures come out of the rocks and weed to feed, and the whiting come in to feed on them.

Use a berley mix of crushed cockle and pieces of squid, but be sure this is kept near the boat. The best way to control the berley flow is to put the berley in chicken wire weighted with a 250-gram sinker. This should be kept about 20 cm from the bottom. By doing this the berley will always be with the boat even if the wind causes it to yaw about. Freshen up the berley every twenty minutes with more squid and cockles so that the smell remains in the water. Baits should be changed every five minutes.

Remember that the bite you feel is not a bite at all; it is the flip of the fish's tail as it swims away with the bait. Therefore you should keep lifting the line slightly to feel the fish's weight and react quickly to the slightest knock on the line. Often this is as light as a leatherjacket bite.

HOW TO COOK

Select two fillets of King George Whiting per person and roll them lightly in breadcrumbs. Heat oil to boiling point in a large frying pan. Place the fillets in the pan for two minutes on each side. The important thing is to cook the fish quickly so that no natural taste or juices are lost.

Sand
Whiting

LOCATION

Southern Queensland, New South Wales, Victoria, northern Tasmania, South Australia, and Western Australia.

DESCRIPTION

Small head, long, slender yet thick body with yellow fins and tail. Also known as Yellowfin Whiting.

BAIT

Sea worms, cockles (pipi), and shrimp. Fresh sea worms are by far the best.

GEAR

From the beaches use a surf rod similar to the Silstar 1200–120BWH and an AT2590 sidecaster. From a boat or jetty the Silstar 1100–90BWS with EX2160 is ideal. The line should be about 4-kg breaking strain. The best rig is a 30-gram sliding sinker above two number 7 limerick hooks on a 1-metre trace.

HOW TO CATCH

It is important to remember that Sand Whiting like warm, shallow waters. This means that most are caught on a rising high tide as the water comes in over the warm sand and exposes small worms and shellfish. At times the schools are in water less than a metre deep. They generally hunt in packs of four or five fish. Dozens of these small packs can be scattered over 100 metres of beach.

Sea worms are their natural food. Bait the hooks so that there is at least 1 cm of tail hanging loose from the hook. Cover the hook right up with the rest of the worm.

Hold the line at all times, as these whiting have a very sharp bite and nine times out of ten they will steal the bait

if the rig is unattended. Strike firmly on the first bite and keep the line tight on the fish all of the time. A slack line with Sand Whiting means a lost fish.

The best time to fish is on the rising high tides at first light and again at dusk. If there is a pier or jetty around, try fishing close to the piles in the shallow water. In some areas in Australia there is only one high tide a day. This will be the one to fish. If the fish are touchy, try moving the bait in short but light jerks so that the sinker disturbs the sand. This little puff of sand will catch the fish's eye and it will move over to investigate the cause. This is when it will see the bait and think a worm has just come out of the sand.

If you have plenty of live worms, try cutting some into 2-cm pieces and dropping them near the line. This will help to bring the fish on to a feeding frenzy.

HOW TO COOK

Take three thin fillets of Sand Whiting or the like and paint them with a butter and garlic paste. Roll the fillets and skewer them with toothpicks. Place the fillets on a shaslik, and separate each fillet with a roll of bacon. Place them under a griller until cooked.

Silver
Whiting

LOCATION

Silver Whiting can be caught around the Australian coast from southern Queensland to Western Australia. It is a school fish and large numbers are netted each year.

DESCRIPTION

Small head and strong body similar to the Sand Whiting. Opaque—silver in colour. Yellow tips of fins and tail.

BAIT

Silver Whiting are essentially worm and shrimp eaters, but they will take cockles (pipi) on occasions. Fresh sea worms are best.

GEAR

A fine tipped rod similar to the Silstar 999—80BWS is essential. This and a mid-range reel like the AT2050 are ideal. Silver Whiting are bottom feeders, therefore the hooks must be below the sinker. Rig two number 7 limerick hooks below a 30-gram pyramid sinker for best results. If you have to cast well out for the fish, try the King George Whiting sliding rig with the smaller hooks.

HOW TO CATCH

Silver Whiting like the warm shallow waters of estuaries and bays, as do Sand Whiting. They are constantly on the move hunting for food. The bulk of this they generally find on the rising high tide, when the sun has killed many small shell creatures and worms.

They react very quickly to the slightest puff of sand on the bottom, and this is why the angler should constantly lift the sinker and let it drop. This action will alert the fish to the baits. Fish as light as possible. A 4-kg breaking strain line is plenty as these fish rarely grow over 1 kg in weight, and most are less than half of this.

Fish in very shallow water as the tide rises, no more than a metre, as this is generally where the fish will be. They like a long sandy or light mud bottom. Hold the rod at all times and keep a tight line.

Silver Whiting have a very fast sharp bite, like the Sand Whiting. It is only a split second, and in that time the bait is gone. If you are fishing from a pier or jetty, try fishing near the piles without any weight at all. Use worms when you try this and leave a long tail on the bait. Cover the hook completely with the remainder of the worm by sliding the hook through the inside of the worm's body.

Keep a wet bag over the fish you have caught, as they go soft very quickly in the heat.

HOW TO COOK

Cut a Silver Whiting into thin, small fillets, about 1 cm deep by 8 cm long and 2 cm wide. This is done by taking pieces from the body of the fish. Roll each fillet in the flour then egg and then the breadcrumbs. Heat cooking oil to near boiling in the frying pan and immerse the fillets. Cook until golden brown. This makes an ideal fish finger which can be eaten immediately or stored in the deep freeze for later use.

Weed Whiting

LOCATION

Southern Australia.

DESCRIPTION

Similar in shape to the King George Whiting. A small head and a slender but thick body. Its colour ranges from bright green to red and brown.

BAIT

Cockles (pipi), crushed squid, worms, and shrimp.

GEAR

Use a light rod similar to the Silstar 999–56BWB and an ST2040 sidecast reel. The line should be about 5-kg breaking strain. Use a sliding sinker rig, a 30-gram between two number 6 limerick hooks. The sinker should be allowed to slide about 40 cm.

HOW TO CATCH

As the name suggests, these fish live in the weed, especially tape weed and posidonia beds. They feed mainly on small crustacea and worms. They are slow movers and give a very sharp bite, more of a pick, when taking a bait. They are found mainly in shallow waters where the weed-line starts. Their flesh is good to eat but when fresh it has a slight iodine taste. A day or two in the refrigerator will overcome this, however.

From a boat, anchor near the edge of a weed patch and throw in plenty of cockle berley. The fish will start to emerge from their weed hideaway. Cover the hooks completely with the baits, usually cockles, but be sure the point is not snagged by any hard meat. Let the Weed Whiting play with the bait. After about the third bite, strike. They have by then got the bait well into their mouth. Keep moving from patch to patch, as there is

rarely more than a dozen fish in each area. They do not school like other whiting.

From the shore, select a spot where the weed-line is within casting distance, and cast right on the edge. There is every chance you could pick up a flathead at the same time. Weed Whiting and flathead often go together. The shore-caster can try two hooks above a berley spring sinker if he finds it hard to draw the fish out of the weed, but be sure to keep fishing near the same spot all of the time or the berley will be wasted.

HOW TO COOK

Take four thin fish cutlets of Weed Whiting and marinate them in a dry white wine for about 10 minutes. Finely dice an onion. Add the onion to a pan of slowly heating butter. Stir and increase the heat and add the fish. Cook either side for about three minutes. Serve the fish and pour the butter and onion over it. This dish can be improved by using broccoli, beans, carrot, and the whole cooked potatoes to give extra colour and enjoyment.

Yabbies

LOCATION

Rivers, dams, and streams in all southern Australian States.

DESCRIPTION

Brown in colour. A mini version of a lobster. Two large nippers, hard shelled body, and a full meaty tail.

BAIT

Meat or fish offal.

GEAR

Two methods can be used. One is a pot and in some states licences are required for their use. The pot is about 60 cm by 30 cm and covered with birdwire. It has two tube-like entrances in either end. The bait is in the centre of the pot. The second method is a simple piece of meat or fish on a string which is thrown into the river or dam near the banks. Pull the lines in slowly every five minutes and use a dab net to lift the clinging yabbies on to the bank.

HOW TO CATCH

Yabbies are one of the most mysterious river creatures in the world. They can appear from nowhere in a river or dam and disappear just as quickly.

The best time to look for yabbies in the River Murray system is just after a flood when all of the backwaters are full. This induces clean, salt-free, cold water to these areas, which is just what the yabbies are looking for.

When using pots, pull them up every 15 minutes and keep replacing the baits, as yabbies rely on smell as much as anything to find their way into the pot.

Keep the yabbies in a wet bag all of the time, and they will still be alive when you get home.

HOW TO COOK

Boil yabbies in salted water; use about a cup of common salt to a medium-sized pot. They should boil for five minutes. Cool them quickly under a running tap. Tear the tail from the yabbies and peel away the shell. Remove the black tube which runs along the back of the tail, and they are then ready to eat. If you want to keep them for a few weeks, put the tails in clean jars with a 50/50 solution of vinegar and water. Add half a teaspoon of salt, four black peppers, and a bay leaf to each jar. Seal the jar. They are then ready for tasty seafood cocktails when you desire.

What & Where?

The following is intended as a quick area guide to the species included in this book which you should be able to catch in each state of Australia.

New South Wales

Shore fishing—Blue Mackerel, Red Mullet, Yellow-eye Mullet, mulloway, salmon, samson fish, snapper, snook, squid, tailor, tommy ruff, trumpeter; *estuaries*—garfish, tarwhine, Sand Whiting, Silver Whiting, Weed Whiting; *rocky areas*—rock cod, Yellowtail Kingfish, leatherjacket, lingfish, parrot fish, trevally

Jetties and piers—Drummer Bream, garfish, Yellowtail Kingfish, Red Mullet, squid, tommy ruff

Tidal sand flats—crabs, flathead, flounder

Tidal rivers, estuaries, bays and gulf waters—Australian Bass, bream, Sea Catfish, flathead, flounder, garfish, Yellow-eye Mullet, mulloway, snook, tarwhine, tommy ruff, trumpeter, Sand Whiting, Silver Whiting, Weed Whiting

Offshore—Blue Mackerel, garfish, Yellowtail Kingfish, Yellow-eye Mullet, mulloway, salmon, snapper, snook, squid, tailor, tarwhine, tommy ruff, trumpeter, tuna, Sand Whiting, Silver Whiting, Weed Whiting; *reef areas*—rock cod, flathead, John Dory, groper, gurnard, leatherjacket, lingfish, Red Mullet, nannygai, parrot fish, red perch, samson fish, Sergeant Baker, squid, trevally

Offshore, northern areas—barracuda, Black Kingfish, Spanish Mackerel, teraglin; *reef areas*—hussar, parrot fish, sweetlip

Freshwater fishing—callop, European Carp, Murray Cod, Freshwater Catfish, redfin perch, silver perch, Brown Trout, Rainbow Trout, yabbies

Northern Territory

Shore fishing—barramundi, rock cod, garfish, Red Mullet, Yellow-eye Mullet, parrot fish, snapper, squid, threadfin, trumpeter

Jetties and piers—garfish, Red Mullet, squid

Tidal rivers, estuaries, bays and gulf waters — barramundi, Sea Catfish, flounder, garfish, Yellow-eye Mullet, threadfin, trumpeter
Offshore — barramundi, garfish, Black Kingfish, Spanish Mackerel, Yellow-eye Mullet, snapper, squid, threadfin, trumpeter, tuna, turrum; *reef areas* — barracuda, crayfish, dart, Red Emperor, groper, hussar, leatherjacket, lingfish, Red Mullet, parrot fish, squid, Coral Trout
Freshwater fishing — callop, Freshwater Catfish

Queensland

Shore fishing — barramundi, garfish, Yellow-eye Mullet, mulloway, snapper, squid, tailor, tarwhine, threadfin, trumpeter; *rocky areas* — rock cod, Yellowtail Kingfish, Red Mullet, parrot fish, samson fish, trevally
Jetties and piers — Yellowtail Kingfish, Red Mullet, squid
Tidal sand flats — crabs, flathead, flounder
Tidal rivers, estuaries, bays and gulf waters — barramundi, Sea Catfish, flathead, flounder, garfish, Yellow-eye Mullet, mulloway, tarwhine, threadfin, trumpeter; *Southern Queensland* — Australian Bass, bream, flathead, garfish, Blue Mackerel, Sand Whiting, Silver Whiting
Offshore — barramundi, garfish, Spanish Mackerel, Yellow-eye Mullet, snapper, squid, tailor, tarwhine, teraglin, threadfin, tuna, turrum; *reef areas* — crayfish, dart, groper, gurnard, hussar, John Dory, Black Kingfish, leatherjacket, lingfish, Red Mullet, nannygai, parrot fish, samson fish, squid, trevally; *tropical reef areas* — barracuda, Red Emperor, flathead, groper, hussar, sweetlip, Coral Trout
Freshwater fishing — callop, Freshwater Catfish, redfin perch

South Australia

Shore fishing — garfish, Blue Mackerel, Yellow-eye Mullet, mulloway, tommy ruff, salmon, snapper, snook, squid, tailor, trumpeter, King George Whiting, Sand Whiting, Silver Whiting, Weed Whiting; *rocky areas* — blackfish, rock cod, Yellowtail Kingfish, Red Mullet, parrot fish, samson fish, sweep, trevally

Piers and jetties — Drummer Bream, garfish, Yellowtail Kingfish, Red Mullet, Jumping Mullet, squid, tommy ruff

Tidal sand flats — crabs, flathead, flounder, Yellow-eye Mullet

Tidal rivers, estuaries, bays and gulf waters — Australian Bass, bream, Sea Catfish, flathead, flounder, garfish, Horse Mackerel, Jumping Mullet, Yellow-eye Mullet, mulloway, Cocktail Shark, snook, tommy ruff, trumpeter, King George Whiting, Sand Whiting, Silver Whiting

Offshore — bonito, salmon, snapper, snook, squid, tailor, tommy ruff, trumpeter, tuna, King George Whiting, Sand Whiting, Silver Whiting, Weed Whiting; *reef areas* — crayfish, dart, flathead, groper, gurnard, John Dory, leatherjacket, lingfish, Blue Morwong, Dusky Morwong, nannygai, parrot fish, red perch, samson fish, Sergeant Baker, Cocktail Shark, squid, trevally

Freshwater fishing — callop, European Carp, Murray Cod, Freshwater Catfish, redfin perch, silver perch, Brown Trout, Rainbow Trout, yabbies

Tasmania

Shore fishing — rock cod, garfish, Blue Mackerel, Red Mullet, Yellow-eye Mullet, mulloway, parrot fish, salmon, snapper, snook, squid, sweep, tailor, tommy ruff, trevally, trumpeter, Weed Whiting; *Northern Tasmania* — blackfish, Yellowtail Kingfish, Sand Whiting, Silver Whiting

Jetties and piers — garfish, Red Mullet, Jumping Mullet, tommy ruff, squid

Tidal rivers, estuaries, bays and gulf waters — Australian Bass, bream, Sea Catfish, flathead, flounder, garfish, Jumping Mullet, Yellow-eye Mullet, mulloway, snook, tommy ruff, trumpeter

Offshore — bonito, nannygai, Cocktail Shark, snapper, snook, squid, tailor, tommy ruff, tuna, Weed Whiting; *reef areas* — crayfish, dart, flathead, groper, gurnard, John Dory, leatherjacket, lingfish, Blue Morwong, nannygai, parrot fish, red perch, Cocktail Shark, squid, trevally

Freshwater fishing — callop, Freshwater Catfish, redfin perch, Brown Trout, Rainbow Trout

Victoria

Shore fishing—blackfish, garfish, Blue Mackerel, Jumping Mullet, Yellow-eye Mullet, mulloway, salmon, snapper, snook, squid, sweep, tailor, tommy ruff, trumpeter, King George Whiting, Sand Whiting, Silver Whiting, Weed Whiting; *rocky areas*—rock cod, Yellowtail Kingfish, Red Mullet, parrot fish, samson fish, trevally

Jetties and piers—Drummer Bream, garfish, Yellowtail Kingfish, Red Mullet, Jumping Mullet, tommy ruff, squid

Tidal rivers, estuaries, bays and gulf waters—bream, Sea Catfish, flathead, flounder, garfish, snook, Horse Mackerel, Jumping Mullet, Yellow-eye Mullet, mulloway, tommy ruff, trumpeter, King George Whiting, Sand Whiting, Silver Whiting; *Western Victoria*—Australian Bass, Cocktail Shark

Offshore—bonito, squid, tailor, tommy ruff, trumpeter, tuna, King George Whiting, Sand Whiting, Silver Whiting, Weed Whiting; *reef areas*—crayfish, dart, flathead, groper, gurnard, John Dory, leatherjacket, lingfish, Blue Morwong, Dusky Morwong, nannygai, parrot fish, red perch, Sergeant Baker, Cocktail Shark, squid, trevally

Freshwater fishing—callop, European Carp, Murray Cod, Freshwater Catfish, redfin perch, silver perch, Brown Trout, Rainbow Trout, yabbies

Western Australia

Shore fishing—barracouta, bream, rock cod, garfish, Yellowtail Kingfish, Red Mullet, Yellow-eye Mullet, mulloway, parrot fish, samson fish, snapper, snook, squid, tailor, tarwhine, trumpeter

Jetties and piers—garfish, Yellowtail Kingfish, Red Mullet, squid, tommy ruff

Tidal sand flats—crabs, flathead, flounder

Tidal rivers, estuaries, bays and gulf waters—bream, Sea Catfish, flathead, flounder, garfish, Yellow-eye Mullet, mulloway, Cocktail Shark, snook, tarwhine, trumpeter

Offshore—barracuda, barracouta, bonito, bream, garfish, Yellow-eye Mullet, snapper, snook, squid, tailor, tarwhine, trumpeter, tuna; *reef areas*—crayfish, dart, dhufish, groper, gurnard, John Dory, leatherjacket, lingfish, Red

Mullet, nannygai, parrot fish, samson fish, Sergeant Baker, squid

Southern Western Australia—Blue Mackerel, Horse Mackerel, Dusky Morwong, salmon, Cocktail Shark, sweep, tommy ruff, King George Whiting, Sand Whiting, Silver Whiting, Weed Whiting

Northern Western Australia—barramundi, Black Kingfish, Spanish Mackerel, threadfin; *reef areas*—Red Emperor, flathead, flounder, groper, hussar, queenfish, teraglin, Coral Trout

Freshwater fishing—callop, Freshwater Catfish, redfin perch; *Southern Western Australia*—Brown Trout, Rainbow Trout

Index